BARITONE / BASS

W9-CCO-642

THE 16-BAR
THEATRE AUDITION

100 SONGS EXCERPTED FOR SUCCESSFUL AUDITIONS

COMPILED AND EDITED BY MICHAEL DANSICKER

ISBN 978-0-634-06443-2

HAL•LEONARD® CORPORATION

7777 W. BLUEMOUND RD. P.O. BOX 13819 MILWAUKEE, WI 53213

Visit Hal Leonard Online at
www.halleonard.com

CONTENTS

*Not from a show

SHOW INDEX

PREFACE

After completing coursework in musical theatre degree programs at universities and conservatories, a very large number of musical theatre graduates, along with other young hopefuls, head for New York City. Their ultimate goal, of course, is a career in the professional musical theatre. Most young actors do not get immediate representation from agents or managers, who can secure for their clients a private appointment with a show's creative team. The standard "open singer's call" has become the most readily available opportunity for thousands of aspiring performers. It provides actors a chance to be heard and considered for work in various venues, from theme park/cruise line shows to Equity Broadway productions.

While directors, choreographers and casting offices are always anxious to discover new talent, audition time continues to be severely limited. Massive turnouts have become "the norm." In order to accommodate the crowds, the audition monitor will frequently announce the casting director's request for a 16-bar excerpt at a singing call. The concept of editing music for auditions becomes a frightening prospect to those not experienced in streamlining their selection on short notice. It is a task that takes musical experience and some careful thought!

WHY 16 BARS?

In the world of popular song writing, the standard 32-bar song form (AABA) has been the backbone of composition for decades. In this context, a 16-bar excerpt would imply half of a song. Prior to about 1970, Broadway shows were vehicles to supply the world with dance tunes and popular music. While the musical selections served the plot and characters of their shows, the songs were also written to have an extended life outside of the theatre. Today there is virtually no crossover from Broadway to the popular music market. Contemporary theatre composers and lyricists do not adhere to traditional structures, commercial form, or content in their work. Their writing faithfully serves the drama they are musicalizing, but it is not easily consolidated for an audition excerpt.

It is not always easy to decide on a 16-bar selection from a song. *The choice should not be arbitrary. You should always choose the best 16 bars!* This could be the verse, the bridge of the song, or an extended coda tagged on to your selected piece. You have to find out what works best for you. Your selection should time between 20 and 30 seconds. *No longer!* In most cases 16 bars is the right amount of music, although occasionally 32 bars will be more appropriate if the selection is in a very fast cut time, or "in 1." If you can communicate effectively to the audition panel in a shorter cutting, such as 8 or 12 bars, then do so! The piano introduction to your singing should be very limited, usually a one-note "bell tone" or one bar. It is not out of line to request your starting pitch when you speak with the pianist. Make sure you clearly communicate the tempo to the audition pianist. Your music should be clearly marked. Any transposition should be neatly written out. Do not expect the accompanist to transpose at sight. Material from showcases, camp shows and college revues should be left at home. Discordant arrangements and bizarre novelty tunes are of little use in 16-bar auditions. Of course, pass over songs that include extended orchestral solos.

BASIC PRESENTATION

You must impart your complete understanding of the music and lyrics you have selected. Your negotiation of the musical phrase and ability to be specific with acting elements are very important. Good singing technique is, of course, essential (placement, breath control and pitch). Your connection with the dramatic integrity of the piece is also important. The song should be presented honestly and thoughtfully. Be familiar with the shows you are auditioning for! Your music should reflect the style and spirit of the musical being cast. Dialects should be avoided; unless told otherwise, sing in English! It is never wise to interpolate unlikely notes to show off the upper limits of your vocal range. If a composer, or a firm performing tradition, has given an optional high note, feel free to use it. However, a disembodied "howl" with no cohesive relation to the phrase will surely not work favorably for you. While the rigor of a competitive audition experience can take its toll, always impart a sense of total commitment to your work, and the joy of being a musical theatre actor.

VOCAL RANGES

On Broadway today, the baritone has become a bari-tenor. A solid high F is imperative; a G is better. Basses should have an audible low F. Sopranos are sometimes asked for high D's, and belters now go as high as F. Tenors many times are asked for high C. But these are the extreme limits of range. At best, a 16-bar selection serves as an introduction to your vocal/acting skills. Do what is comfortable for you. If you are to be considered for a position in a production, further exploration of your vocal ability will take place in a callback situation. *You can't show everything in 16 bars!* Tenors should feel free to use selections from the baritone volume. Ladies should be ready to show the legit (soprano) and belt aspects of their voices if asked. Always have an alternate selection ready.

DANCERS

The dancer's call is a bit different than an open singer's call. The singing portion of the dancer audition is held only after the dancers have learned the presented movement combination and made their way through an elimination process. While many dancers in New York can hold their own at any singer call, the creative team will be a bit more flexible with dancers for the singing portion of the audition.

THE SELECTIONS IN THESE VOLUMES

The repertoire of the Broadway musical remains abundant and diversified, but large segments of material remain under-utilized. I have included selections from Broadway musicals, operettas, and pop hits. I gravitated to writers of outstanding talent and exceptional merit. A well-written song is a tremendous asset to any performer. No individual will be able to use all 100 excerpts in a particular anthology! There are songs that demand leading lady and leading man stature, as well as character and comic selections. There are pieces that have enormous vocal range, and many that are just rhythmic and charming. It is your job to peruse the contents and find what you consider the right songs for your needs. I have heard all of this material used to great advantage at many auditions. I have attempted to edit and indicate the most effective cuttings, trying to avoid phrase interruption. I have chosen what I feel are the most suitable keys, however, do not be afraid to experiment with the key (but have it written out to take to the audition!). Do not be afraid to use a song that is commonly heard at auditions. It is important that your "take" on the material be intelligent and professional. Every actor is unique, and those listening to your audition will not object to hearing a song again.

AUDITIONING

The only way to secure a job in legitimate musical theatre is through a live audition. Everyone auditions! Some actors audition better than others. The audition process is one that takes time to hone, polish and perfect. While many successful film and television actors secure continuous employment via a compilation reel of their media exposure, stage actors must book via a live audition. Be honest in evaluating the success of each audition, and study how it can be improved in the future. Also take note of the people you are auditioning for, and keep this information in a journal for future reference. Continue studying voice and working with a vocal coach. Dance and acting classes are essential for keeping your work sharp and at a high, professional level.

I hope these editions of 16-bar selections will be helpful to actors planning to audition for any musical show. *It is very important that you also learn the entire song after you master the 16-bar excerpt.* There is always a chance that someone on the creative team will say, "That was great; let's hear the whole song!" *Be prepared.*

Michael Dansicker
New York City
December, 2003

MICHAEL DANSICKER has worked as arranger, composer, musical director, and pianist on over 100 Broadway and Off-Broadway productions, from *Grease* (1975) to *Dance of the Vampires* (2003). He has composed original music for over a dozen plays in New York, including *The Glass Menagerie* (revival with Jessica Tandy) and *Total Abandon* (with Richard Dreyfus), and musically supervised the Royal Shakespeare Company transfers of *Piaf*, *Good*, and *Les Liaisons Dangereuses*. He served as vocal consultant to the hit films *Elf* (New Line Cinema), *Analyze That!* (Warner Bros.), and *Meet the Parents* (Universal), and also scored the dance sequences for Paramount's comedy classic *Brain Donors* (starring John Turturro). In the world of concert dance, he has composed and scored pieces for Twyla Tharp, American Ballet Theatre, Geoffrey Holder, Mikhail Baryshnikov, and The Joffrey, as well as serving as pianist to Jerome Robbins and Agnes DeMille. Michael currently works as creative consultant to Walt Disney Entertainment. He composed the music for "The Audition Suite" (lyrics by Martin Charnin), published by Hal Leonard Corporation. As a vocal coach, he works with the top talent in New York and Hollywood (including Sony's pop division). As an audition pianist, he works regularly with important casting directors on both coasts, and for 15 years has played all major auditions for Jay Binder, the "dean" of Broadway casting. Mr. Dansicker's original music is licensed by BMI. He holds a MA from the Catholic University of America.

Excerpt

ALL I CARE ABOUT
from *Chicago*

Words by FRED EBB
Music by JOHN KANDER

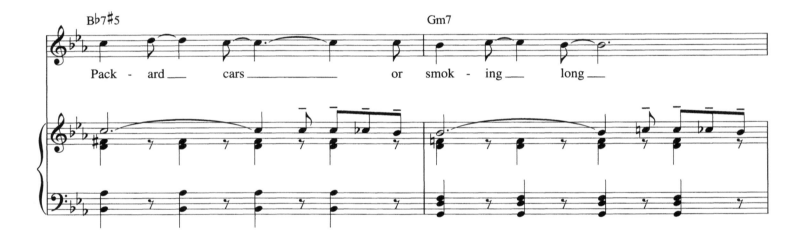

For the complete song see: HL00740125 *The Singer's Musical Theatre Anthology, Baritone/Bass Vol. 3*, and other sources.

All I care a-bout is do-in' a guy in ___ who's

pick-in' on you. Twist-in' the wrist ___ that's

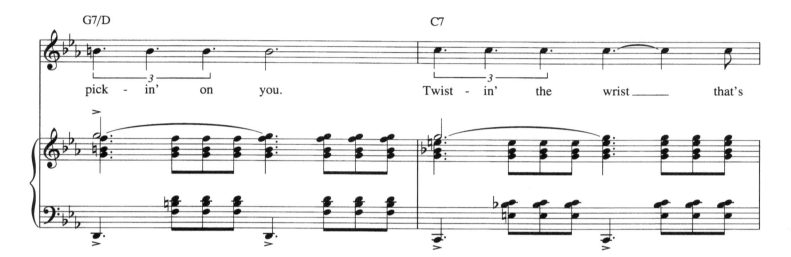

turn-in' the screw. ___ All I care a-bout is ___

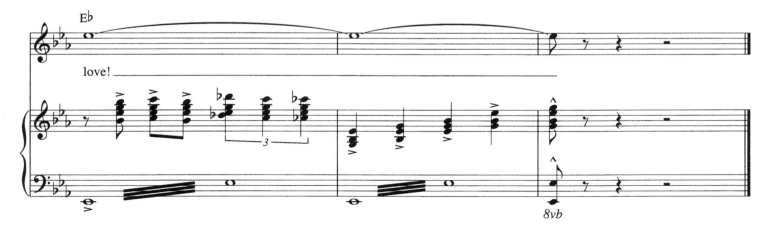

love! ___

Excerpt

ALL I NEED IS THE GIRL

from *Gypsy*

Words by STEPHEN SONDHEIM
Music by JULE STYNE

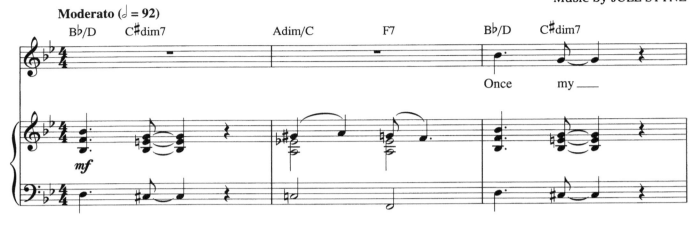

For the complete song see: HL00312187 *Gypsy* vocal selections, and other sources.

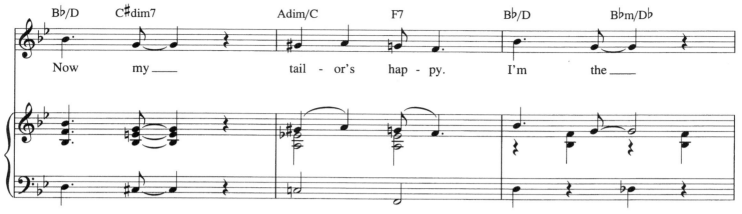

Now my ___ tail - or's hap - py. I'm the ___

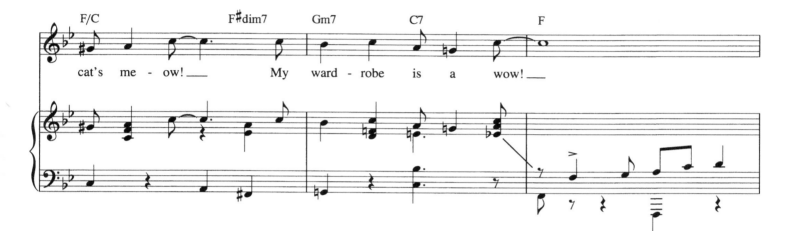

cat's me - ow! ___ My ward - robe is a wow! ___

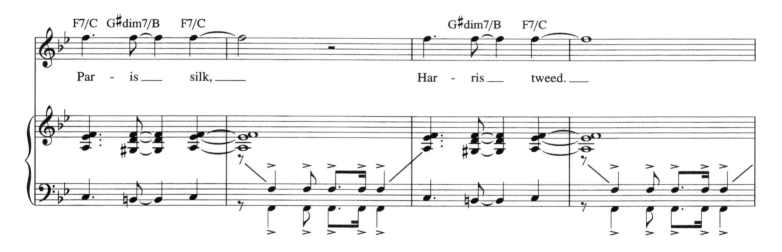

Par - is ___ silk, ___ Har - ris ___ tweed. ___

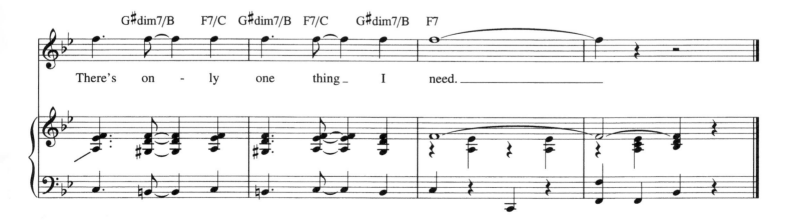

There's on - ly one thing ___ I need. ___

ALL OF YOU
from *Silk Stockings*

Words and Music by
COLE PORTER

For the complete song see: HL00747033 *The Singer's Musical Theatre Anthology, Baritone/Bass Vol. 2*, and other sources.

Excerpt

ANYWHERE I WANDER
from the Motion Picture *Hans Christian Andersen*

By FRANK LOESSER

For the complete song see: HL00747069 *The Singer's Movie Anthology, Men's Edition,* and other sources.

ALONE AT THE DRIVE-IN MOVIE

Excerpt

from *Grease*

Lyric and Music by WARREN CASEY
and JIM JACOBS

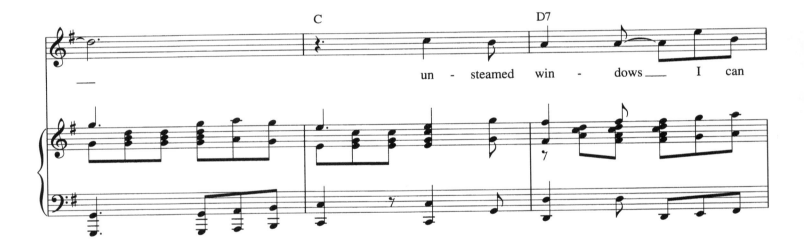

For the complete song see: HL00383674 *Grease* vocal selections, and other sources.

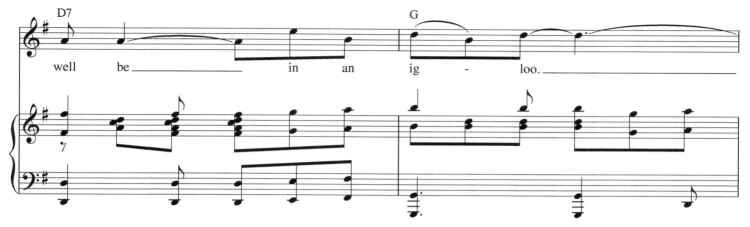

well be _____ in an ig - loo. _____

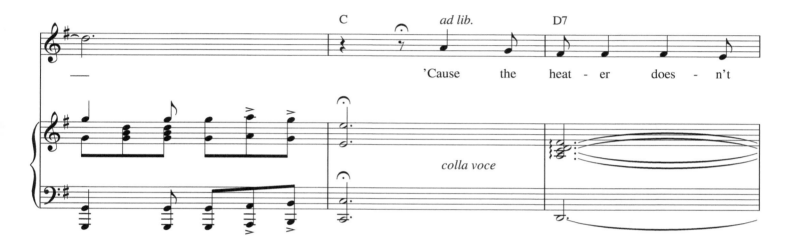

___ 'Cause the heat - er does - n't

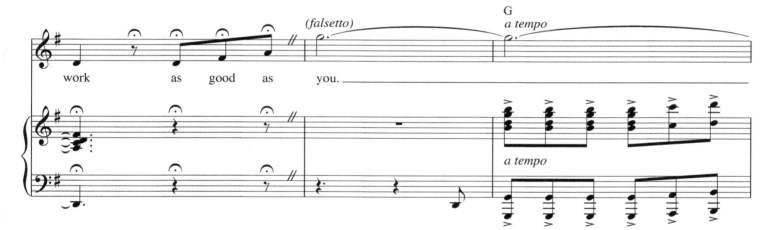

work as good as you. _____

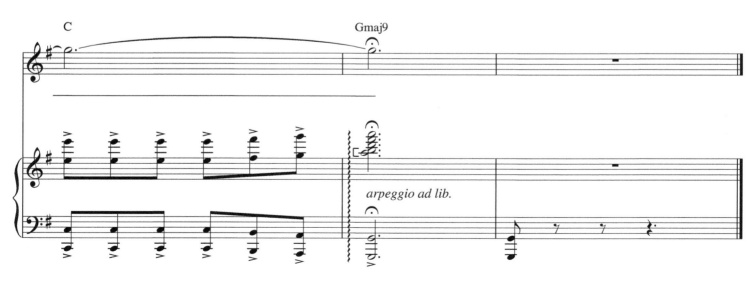

Excerpt

(Walking)
AMONG MY YESTERDAYS
from *The Happy Time*

Words by FRED EBB
Music by JOHN KANDER

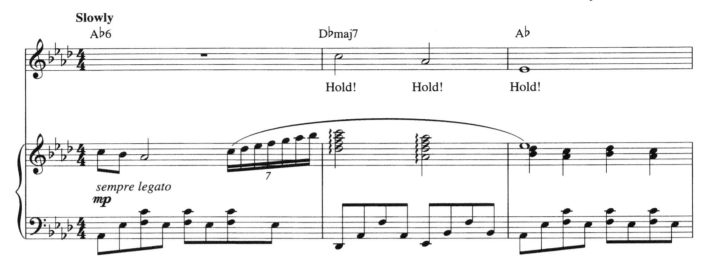

Hold! Hold! Hold!

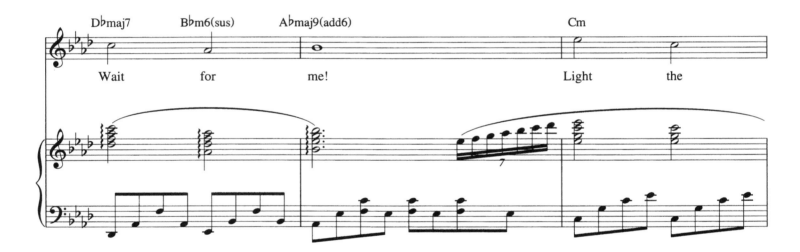

Wait for me! Light the

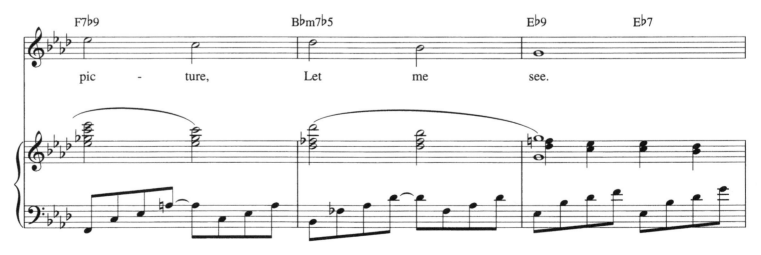

pic - ture, Let me see.

Souvenirs of the past remain. Bits of pleasure and

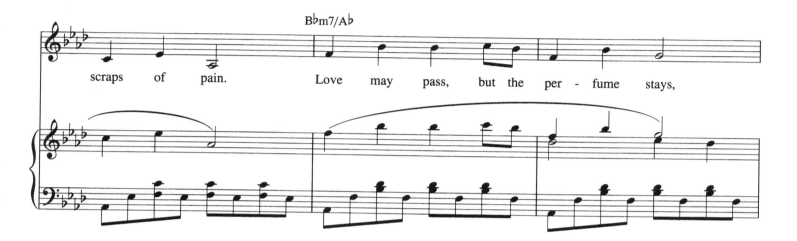

scraps of pain. Love may pass, but the perfume stays,

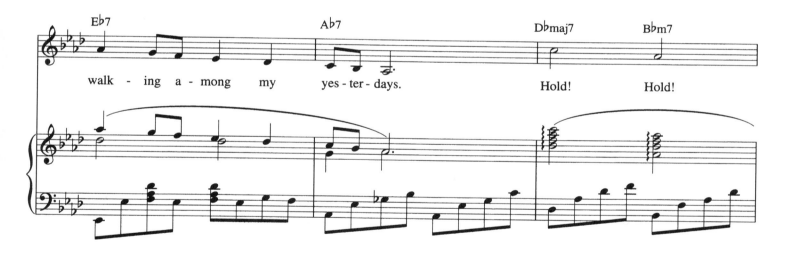

walk-ing a-mong my yes-ter-days. Hold! Hold!

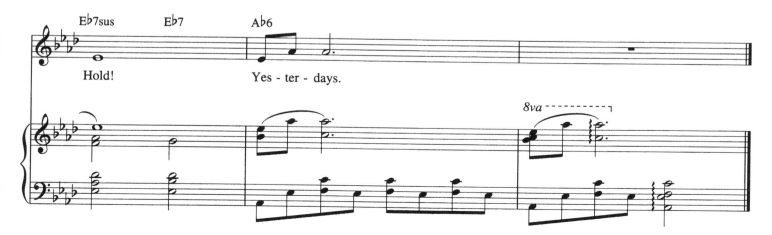

Hold! Yes-ter-days.

Excerpt

BEING ALIVE
from *Company*

Music and Lyrics by
STEPHEN SONDHEIM

For the complete song see: HL00359494 *Company* vocal selections, and other sources.

vive _____ Be - ing a - live, _____

Be - ing a - live, _____ Be - ing a - live! _____

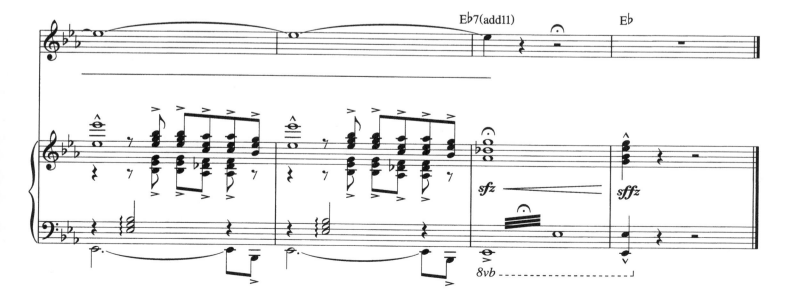

BLOW HIGH, BLOW LOW
from *Carousel*

Lyrics by OSCAR HAMMERSTEIN II
Music by RICHARD RODGERS

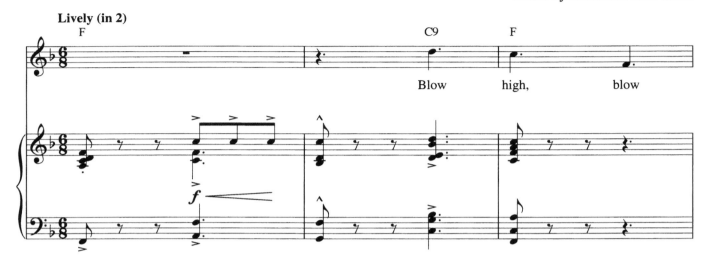

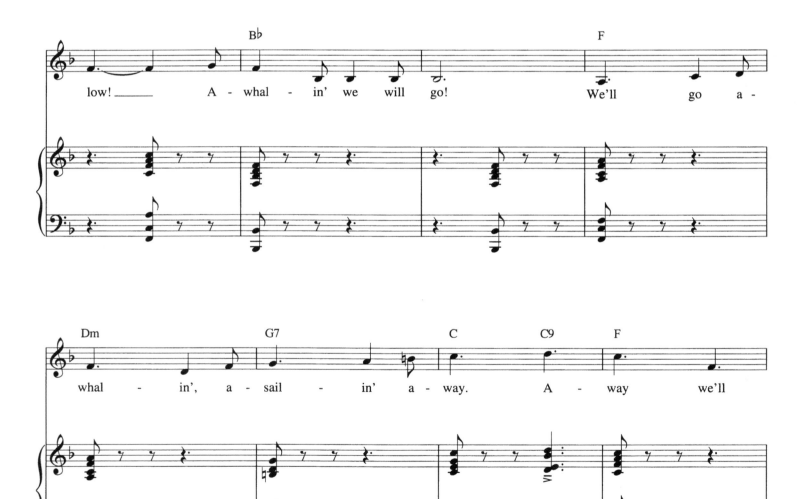

For the complete song see: HL00631193 *TheRodgers & Hammerstein CD-ROM Sheet Music.*

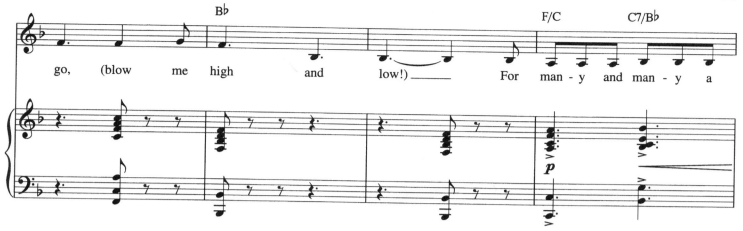

go, (blow me high and low!) _____ For man-y and man-y a

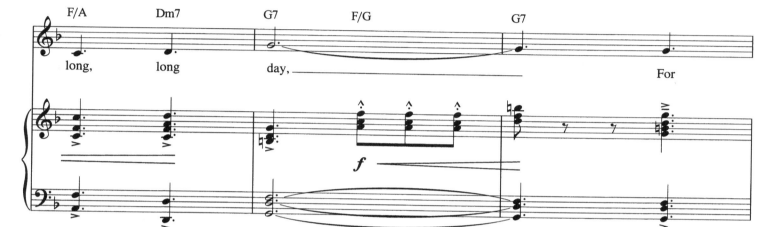

long, long day, _____ For

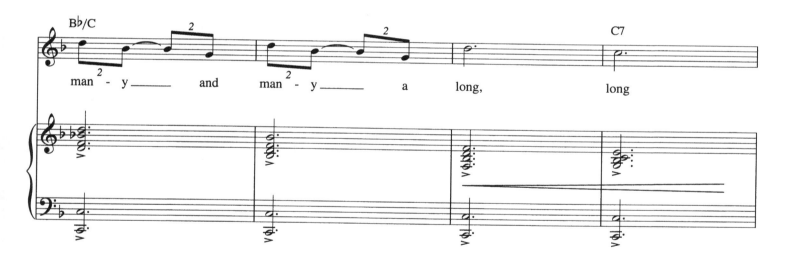

man-y _____ and man-y _____ a long, long

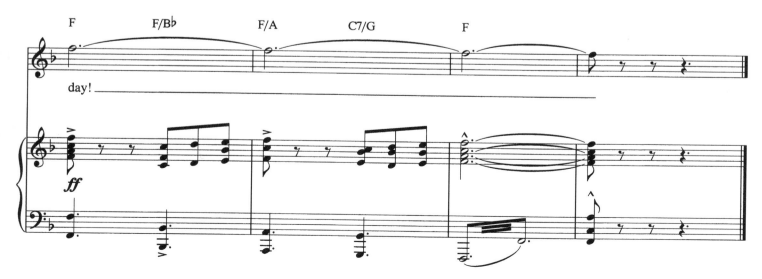

day! _____

Excerpt

BRING ME MY BRIDE
from *A Funny Thing Happened on the Way to the Forum*

Words and Music by
STEPHEN SONDHEIM

For the complete song see: HL00312152 *A Funny Thing Happened on the Way to the Forum* vocal score.

BUDDY'S BLUES
from *Follies*

Words and Music by
STEPHEN SONDHEIM

For the complete song see: HL00740124 *The Singer's Musical Theatre Anthology, Tenor Vol. 3,* and other sources.

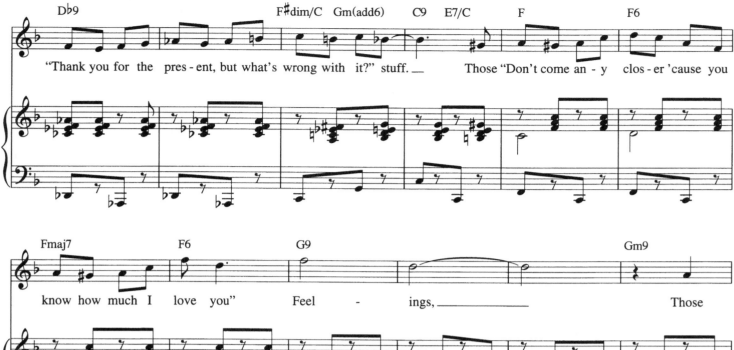

"Thank you for the pres-ent, but what's wrong with it?" stuff. __ Those "Don't come an-y clos-er 'cause you

know how much I love you" Feel - ings, __ Those

"Tell me that you love me, oh you did, I got-ta run now" Blues! __

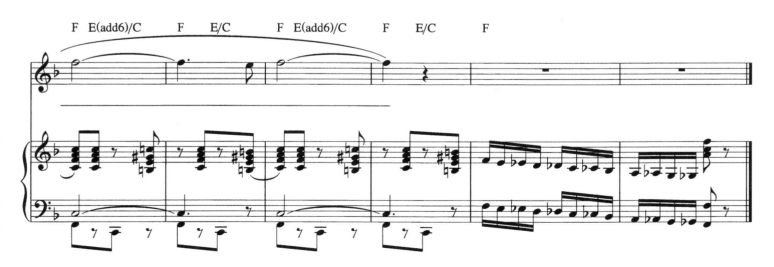

Excerpt

C'EST MOI
from *Camelot*

Words by ALAN JAY LERNER
Music by FREDERICK LOEWE

For the complete song see: HL00361074 *The Singer's Musical Theatre Anthology, Baritone/Bass Vol. 1 (Revised)*, and other sources.

Excerpt

CAN'T HELP FALLING IN LOVE

from the Paramount Picture *Blue Hawaii*

Words and Music by GEORGE DAVID WEISS,
HUGO PERETTI and LUIGI CREATORE

Moderately slow

Like a riv-er flows sure-ly to the sea, dar-ling, so it goes some things _ are meant to be. Take my hand, take my whole life

too, _ For I can't help fall-ing in love with you, _ For

I can't help fall-ing in love with you. _

For the complete song see: HL00303359 *Can't Help Falling in Love* piano/vocal sheet music, and other sources.

Excerpt

COLORADO, MY HOME
from Meredith Willson's *The Unsinkable Molly Brown*

Words and Music by
MEREDITH WILLSON

For the complete song see: HL00447210 *The Unsinkable Molly Brown* vocal selections.

Excerpt

COME BACK TO ME
from *On a Clear Day You Can See Forever*

Words by ALAN JAY LERNER
Music by BURTON LANE

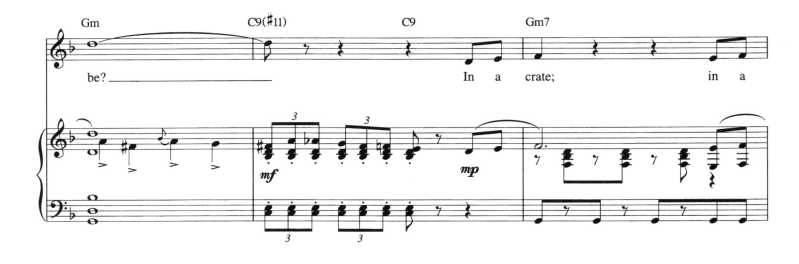

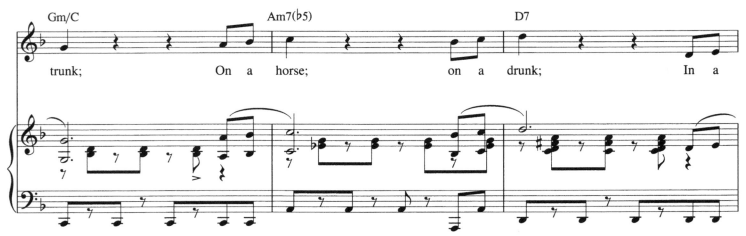

For the complete song see: HL00740125 *The Singer's Musical Theatre Anthology, Baritone/Bass Vol. 3*, and other sources.

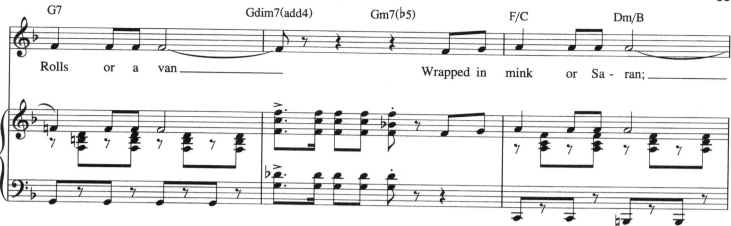

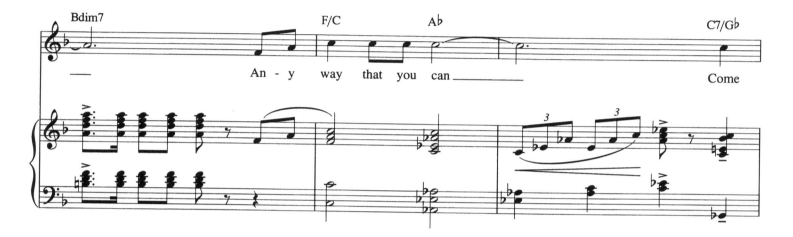

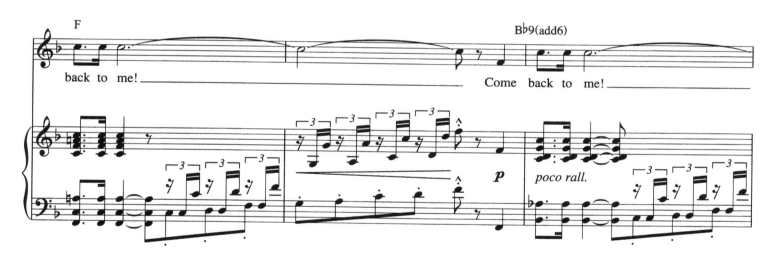

Excerpt

CELEBRATION
from *Celebration*

Words by TOM JONES
Music by HARVEY SCHMIDT

For the complete song see: HL00312070 *Celebration* vocal selections.

Excerpt

DO I LOVE YOU BECAUSE YOU'RE BEAUTIFUL?

from *Cinderella*

Lyrics by OSCAR HAMMERSTEIN II
Music by RICHARD RODGERS

For the complete song see: HL00361074 *The Singer's Musical Theatre Anthology, Baritone/Bass Vol. 1 (Revised)*, and other sources.

Excerpt

DEAR OLD SYRACUSE
from *The Boys from Syracuse*

Words by LORENZ HART
Music by RICHARD RODGERS

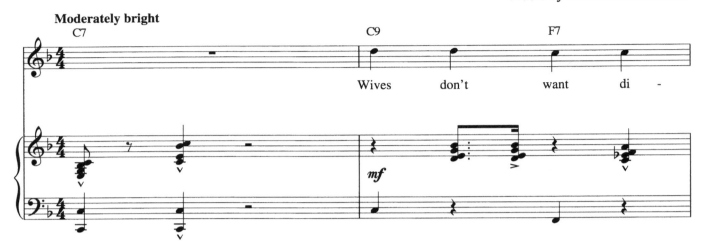

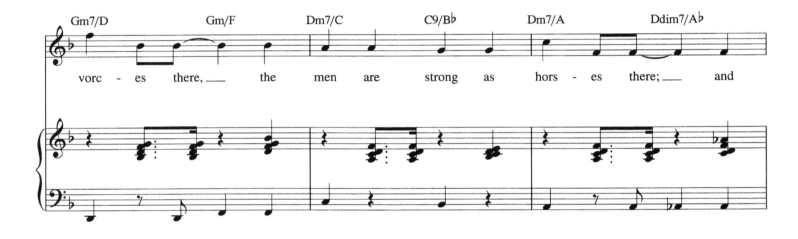

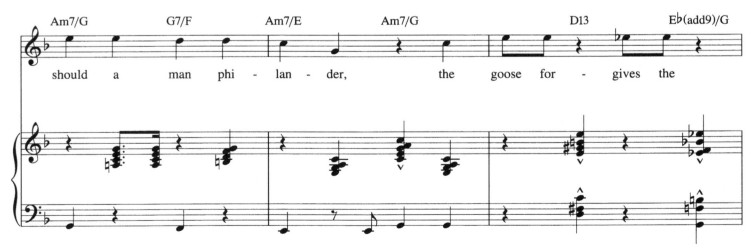

For the complete song see: HL00312046 *The Boys from Syracuse* vocal score.

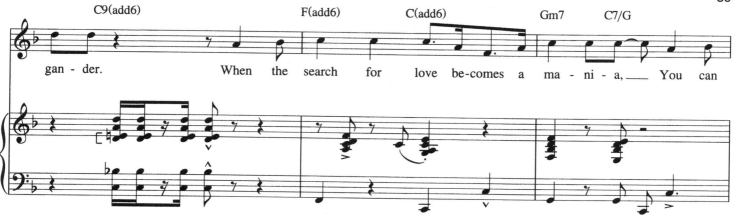

gan - der. When the search for love be-comes a ma - ni - a, ___ You can

take the night boat to Al - ba - ni - a! I want to go back... go

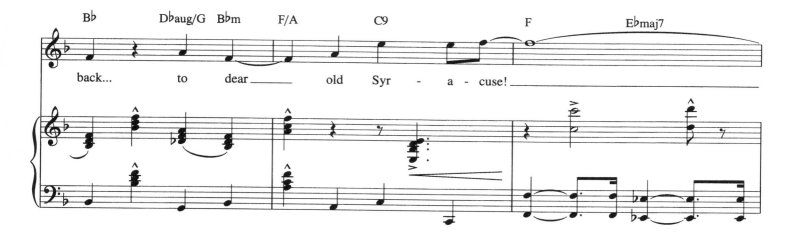

back... to dear ___ old Syr - a - cuse! ___

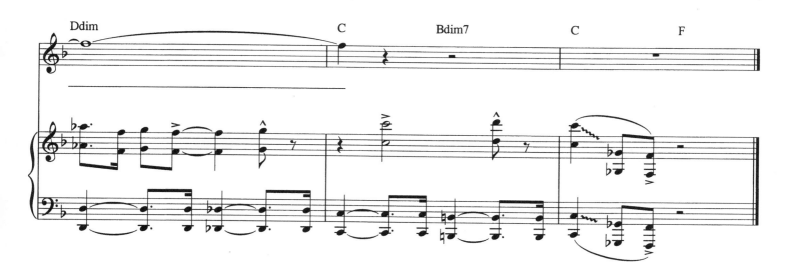

Excerpt

DON'T GET AROUND MUCH ANYMORE

from *Sophisticated Ladies*

Words and Music by DUKE ELLINGTON
and BOB RUSSELL

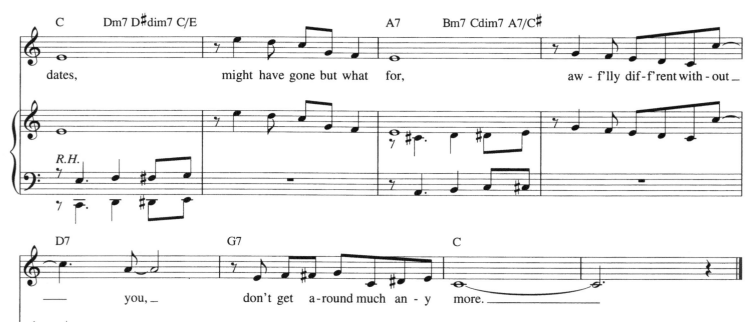

For the complete song see: HL00306011 *Duke Ellington: An American Composer,* and other sources.

A FELLOW NEEDS A GIRL
from *Allegro*

Lyrics by OSCAR HAMMERSTEIN II
Music by RICHARD RODGERS

When things go right and his job's well done, he wants to share the prize he's won. If no one shares, and no one cares, where's the fun of a job well done? Or a prize you've won? A fel-low needs a home, his own kind of home, But to make this dream come true, A fel-low needs a girl, his own kind of girl. My kind of girl is you!

For the complete song see: HL00312007 *Allegro* vocal selections, and other sources.

EMPTY CHAIRS AT EMPTY TABLES

from *Les Misérables*

Music by CLAUDE-MICHEL SCHÖNBERG
Lyrics by ALAIN BOUBLIL and HERBERT KRETZMER

For the complete song see: HL00747033 *The Singer's Musical Theatre Anthology, Baritone/Bass Vol. 2*, and other sources.

Oh my friends, my friends don't ask me _____

what your sac - ri - fice was for. _____ Emp - ty chairs at emp - ty

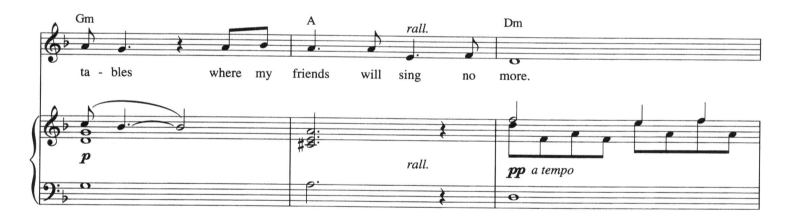

ta - bles where my friends will sing no more.

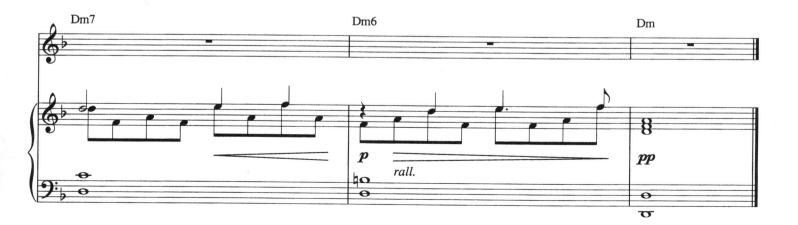

GET ME TO THE CHURCH ON TIME

Excerpt

from *My Fair Lady*

Words by ALAN JAY LERNER
Music by FREDERICK LOEWE

For the complete song see: HL00312265 *My Fair Lady* vocal selections, and other sources.

don't lose the com-pass; And get me to the

church. Get me to the church. For

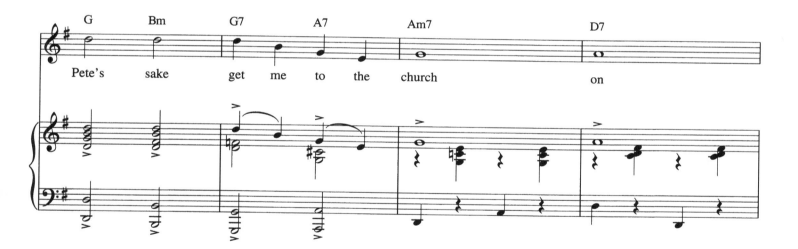

Pete's sake get me to the church on

time!

Excerpt

HEAVEN'S LIGHT
from Walt Disney's *The Hunchback of Notre Dame*

Music by ALAN MENKEN
Lyrics by STEPHEN SCHWARTZ

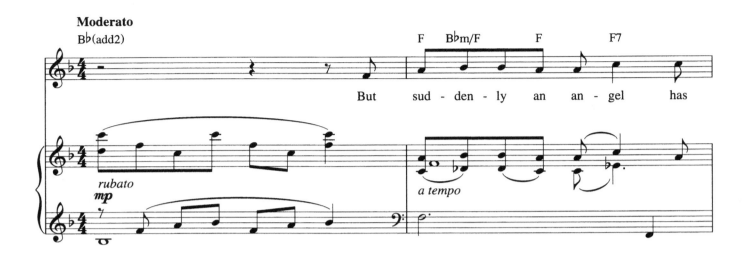

For the complete song see: HL00313045 *The Hunchback of Notre Dame* vocal selections, and other sources.

night   my cold dark tow - er seems so bright.

I swear it must be heav-en's light. _____

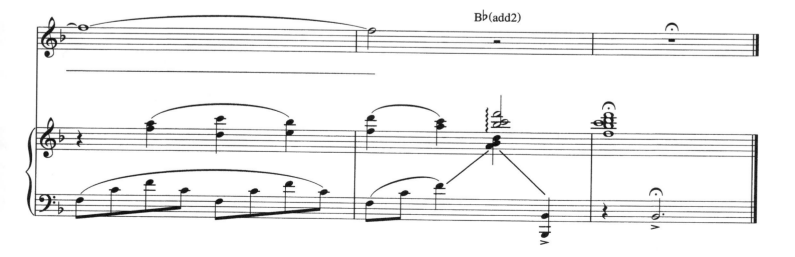

HABEN SIE GEHÖRT DAS DEUTSCHE BAND?

(Have You Ever Heard the German Band?)

from *The Producers*

Music and Lyrics by
MEL BROOKS

For the complete song see: HL00313189 *The Producers* vocal selections, and other sources.

Excerpt

I COULD WRITE A BOOK

from *Pal Joey*

Words by LORENZ HART
Music by RICHARD RODGERS

Allegretto - in 2

And the sim - ple se - cret of the plot _____ Is just to tell them that I love you a lot. _____ Then the world dis - cov - ers, as my book ends, How to make two lov - ers of friends.

For the complete song see: HL00312313 *Pal Joey* vocal selections, and other sources.

I CAN SEE IT
from *The Fantasticks*

Words by TOM JONES
Music by HARVEY SCHMIDT

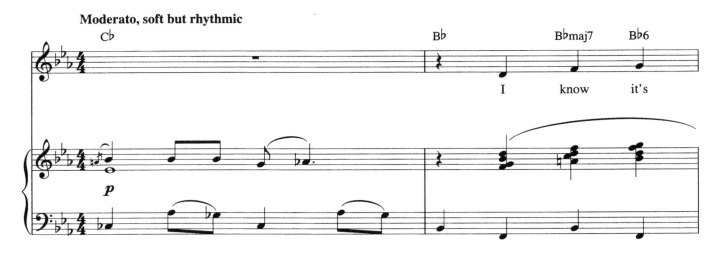

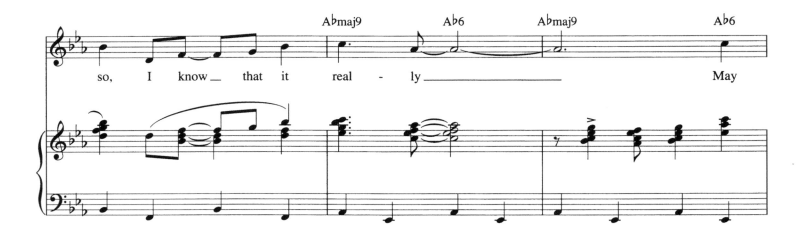

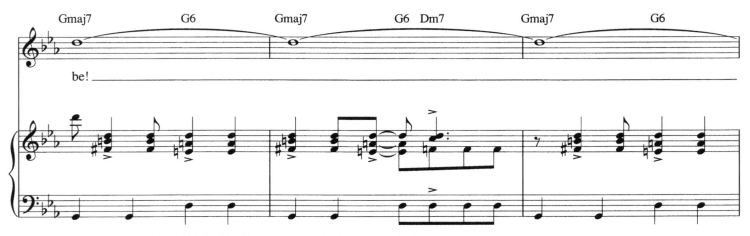

For the complete song see: HL00312136 *The Fantasticks* vocal selections, and other sources.

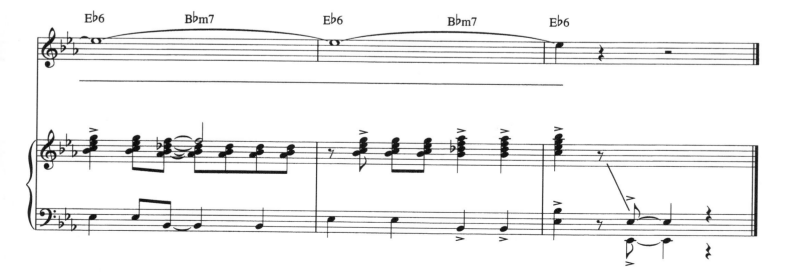

I DON'T REMEMBER YOU
from *The Happy Time*

Words by FRED EBB
Music by JOHN KANDER

For the complete song see: HL00740125 *The Singer's Musical Theatre Anthology, Baritone/Bass Vol. 3*, and other sources.

Excerpt

I WANT TO BE WITH YOU
from *Golden Boy*

Lyric by LEE ADAMS
Music by CHARLES STROUSE

We're gon-na have it all! I'll love you ev-'ry day! Hon-ey, life could be so great for us. Here's our chance, it's not too late for us. Grab it fast or life won't wait for us I wan-na be with you! I wan-na be with you!

For the complete song see: HL00313247 *Songs of Charles Strouse*.

Excerpt

I HAVE DREAMED
from *The King and I*

Lyrics by OSCAR HAMMERSTEIN II
Music by RICHARD RODGERS

Slowly, with much expression

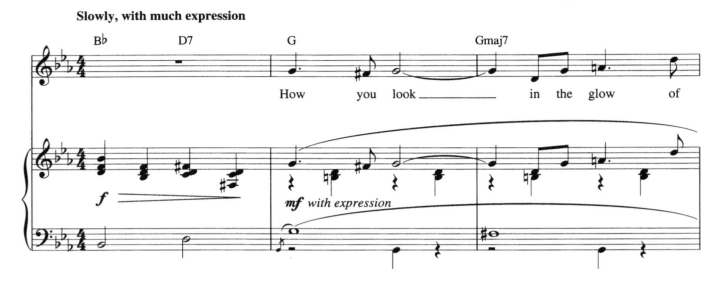

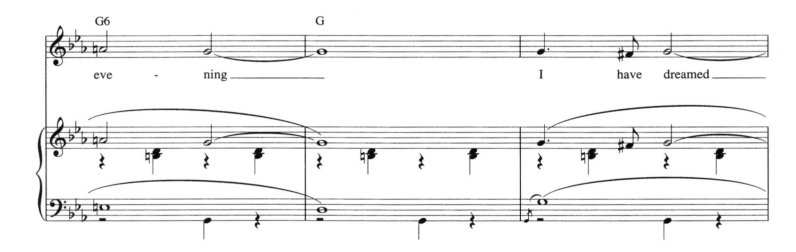

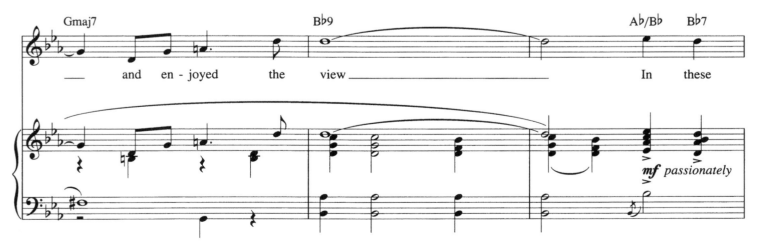

For the complete song see: HL00312227 *The King and I* vocal selections, and other sources.

dreams I've loved you so that by now I think I

know what it's like to be loved by

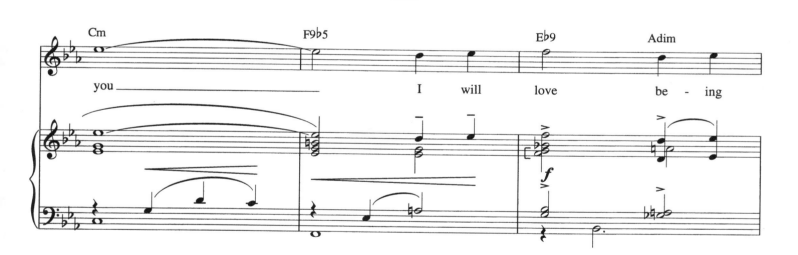

you _____ I will love be - ing

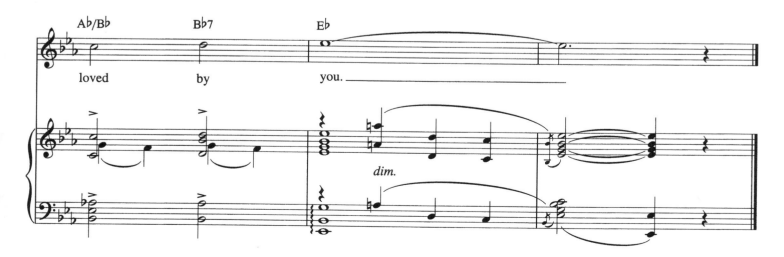

loved by you. _____

I KNOW ABOUT LOVE
from *Do Re Mi*

Words by BETTY COMDEN and ADOLPH GREEN
Music by JULE STYNE

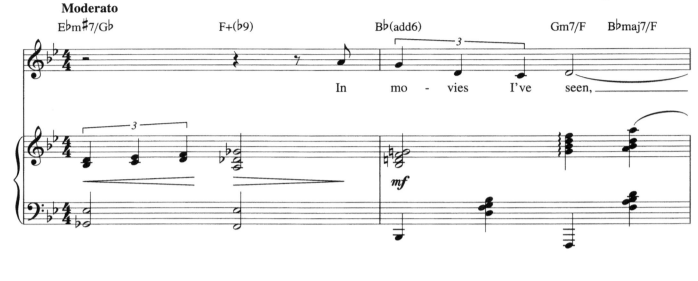

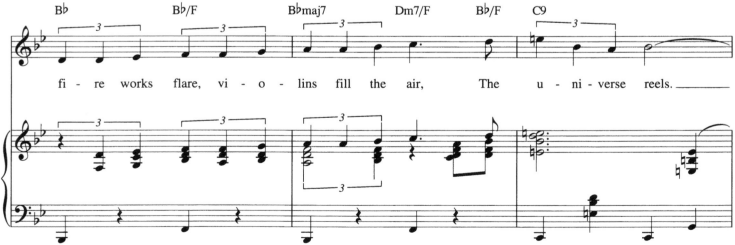

For the complete song see: HL00747032 *The Singer's Musical Theatre Anthology, Tenor Vol. 2.*

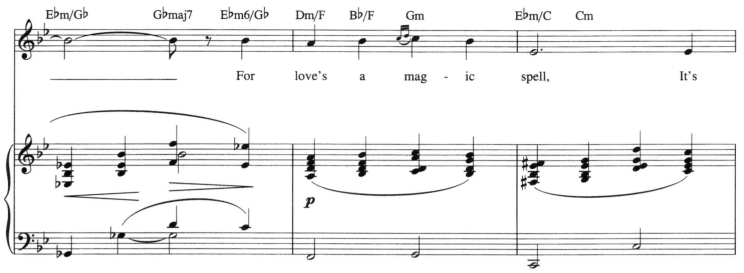

For love's a mag - ic spell, It's

what makes mu - sic sell. I know all a - bout it,

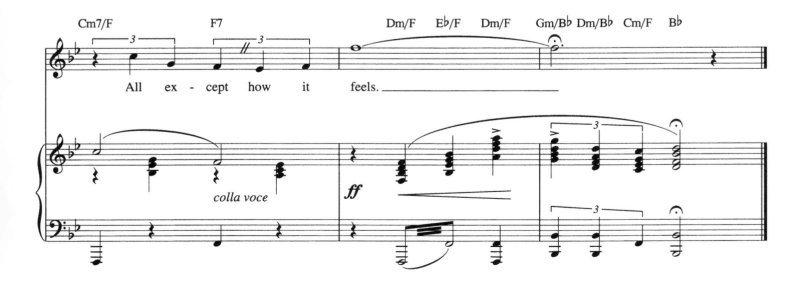

All ex - cept how it feels.

Excerpt

I MET A GIRL
from *Bells Are Ringing*

Words by BETTY COMDEN and ADOLPH GREEN
Music by JULE STYNE

For the complete song see: HL00747032 *The Singer's Musical Theatre Anthology, Tenor Vol. 2.*

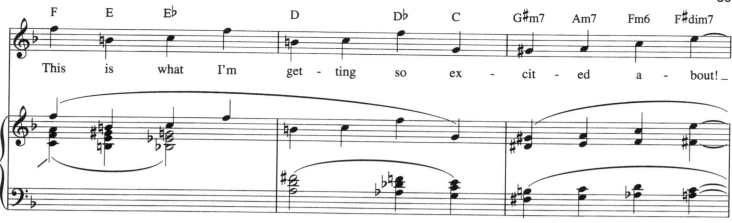

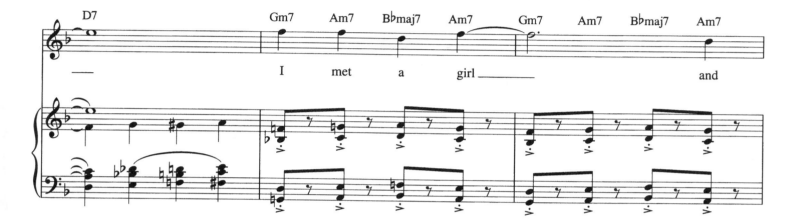

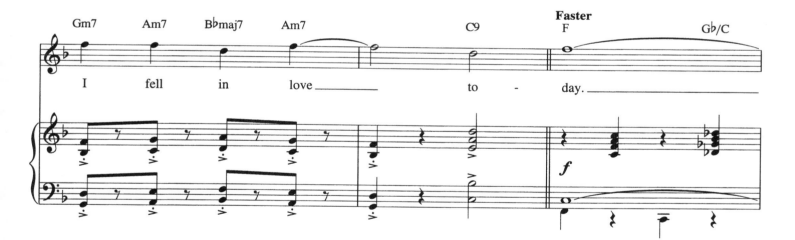

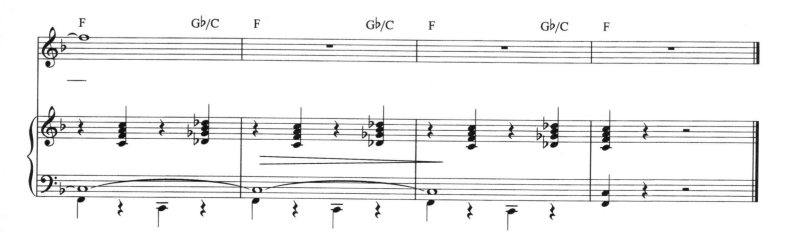

Excerpt

I WISH I WERE IN LOVE AGAIN

from *Babes in Arms*

Words by LORENZ HART
Music by RICHARD RODGERS

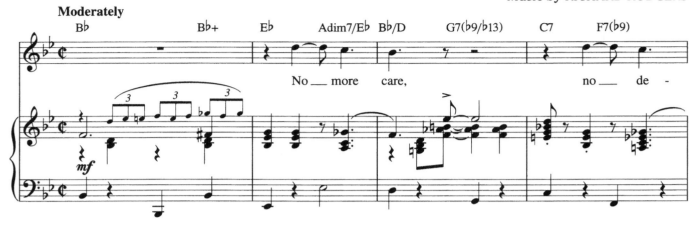

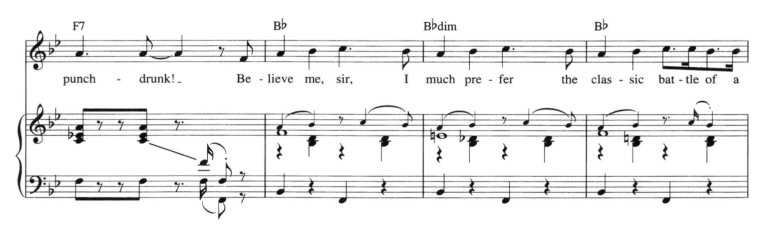

For the complete song see: HL00740167 *The Songs of Richard Rodgers – Low Voice*, and other sources.

Excerpt

I WON'T SEND ROSES
from *Mack and Mabel*

Music and Lyric by
JERRY HERMAN

Moderato

In me you'll find things like guts and nerve,
But not the kind things that you de - serve. And so while
there's a fight-ing chance just turn and go. I won't send ros - es
And ros - es suit you so. _____

For the complete song see: HL00747033 *The Singer's Musical Theatre Anthology, Baritone/Bass Vol. 2,* and other sources.

I'LL BUILD A STAIRWAY TO PARADISE

from *George White's Scandals of 1922*
from *An American in Paris*

Words by B.G. DeSYLVA and IRA GERSHWIN
Music by GEORGE GERSHWIN

For the complete song see: HL00311642 *100 Years of Broadway*, and other sources.

Excerpt

I'LL NEVER SAY NO
from *The Unsinkable Molly Brown*

Words and Music by
MEREDITH WILLSON

For the complete song see: HL00747033 *The Singer's Musical Theatre Anthology, Baritone/Bass Vol. 2,* and other sources.

I'VE JUST SEEN HER
(As Nobody Else Has Seen Her)
from *All American*

Lyric by LEE ADAMS
Music by CHARLES STROUSE

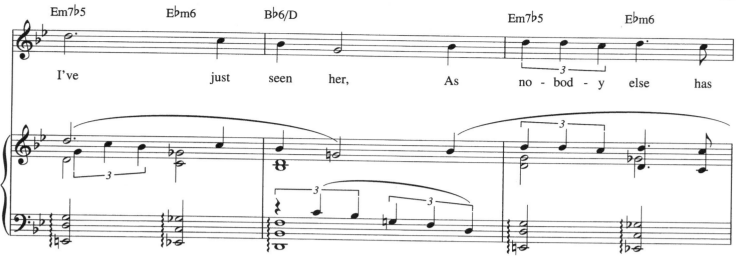

I've just seen her, As no-bod-y else has

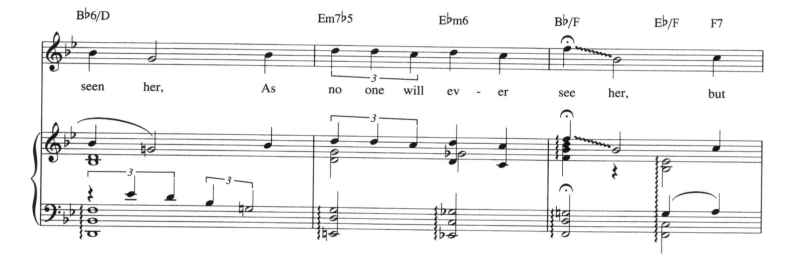

seen her, As no one will ev-er see her, but

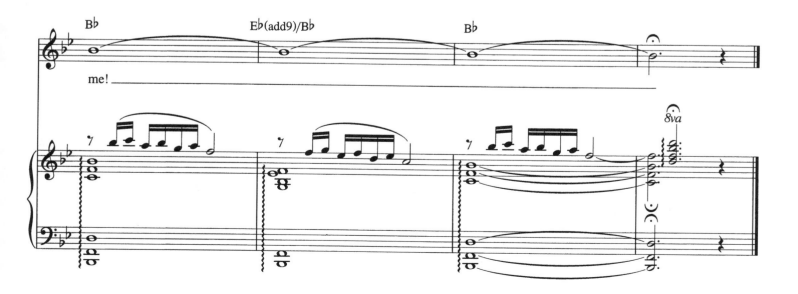

me! _____

Excerpt

IF EVER I WOULD LEAVE YOU

from *Camelot*

Words by ALAN JAY LERNER
Music by FREDERICK LOEWE

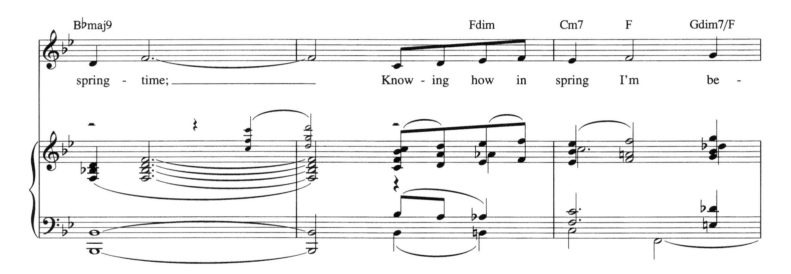

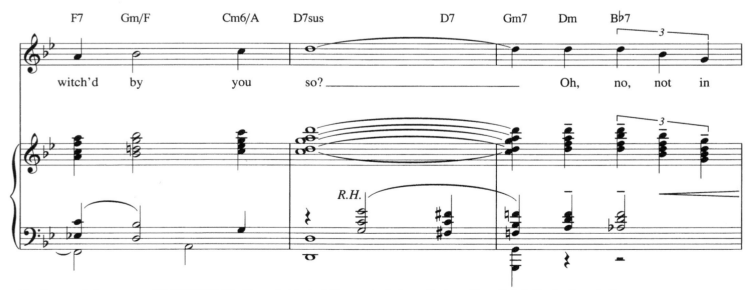

For the complete song see: HL00361074 *The Singer's Musical Theatre Anthology, Baritone/Bass Vol. 1 (Revised)*, and other sources.

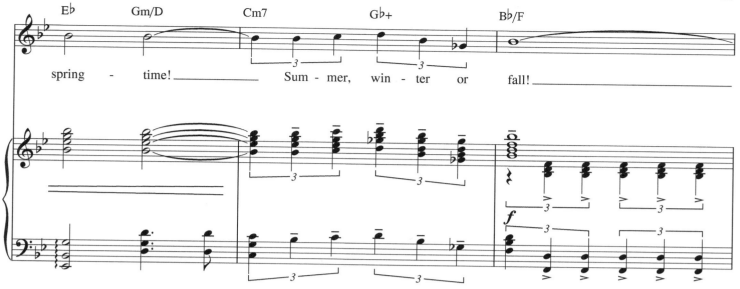

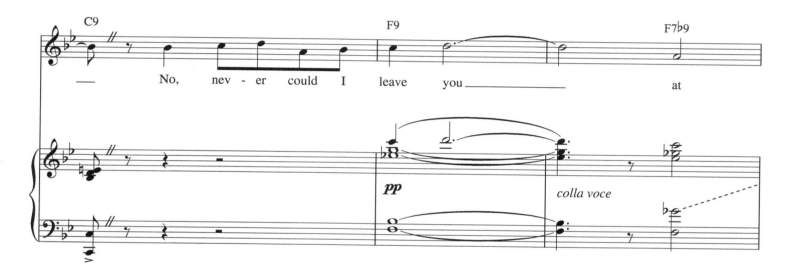

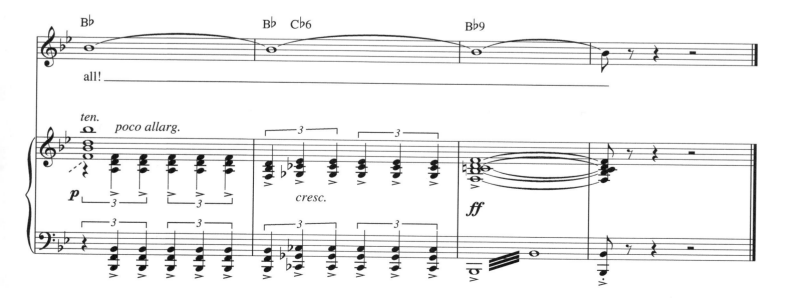

Excerpt

IF I CAN'T LOVE HER

from Walt Disney's *Beauty and the Beast: The Broadway Musical*

Music by ALAN MENKEN
Lyrics by TIM RICE

For the complete song see: HL00740125 *The Singer's Musical Theatre Anthology, Baritone/Bass Vol. 3,* and other sources.

not to be. If I can't love

her, _____ let the world be done with

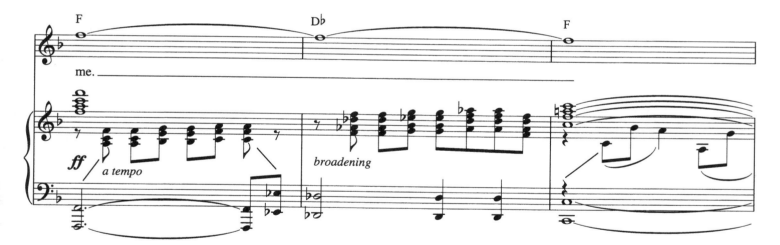

me. _____

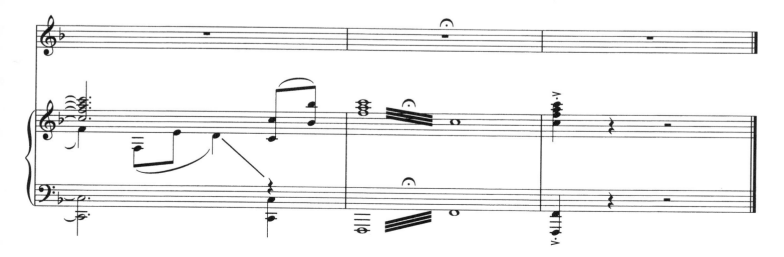

IF I LOVED YOU
from *Carousel*

Lyrics by OSCAR HAMMERSTEIN II
Music by RICHARD RODGERS

Slowly, with great warmth

For the complete song see: HL00361074 *The Singer's Musical Theatre Anthology, Baritone/Bass Vol. 1 (Revised),* and other sources.

THE IMPOSSIBLE DREAM
(The Quest)
from *Man of La Mancha*

Lyric by JOE DARION
Music by MITCH LEIGH

Tempo di Bolero (not too slow)

And I know, _____ if I'll on-ly be

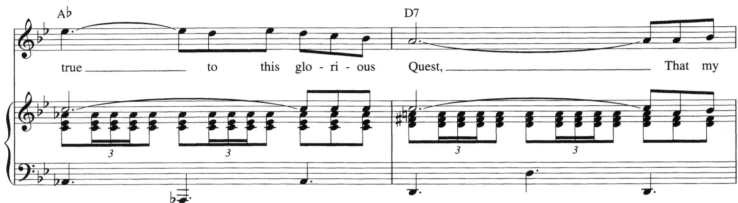

true _____ to this glo-ri-ous Quest, _____ That my

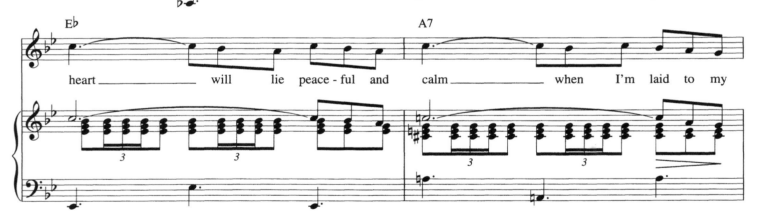

heart _____ will lie peace-ful and calm _____ when I'm laid to my

rest. And the world _____ will be bet-ter for

For the complete song see: HL00361074 *The Singer's Musical Theatre Anthology, Baritone/Bass Vol. 1 (Revised)*, and other sources.

this, _____ That one man, _____ scorned and cov - ered with

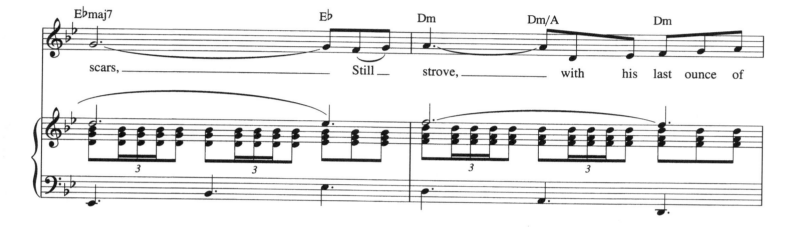

scars, _____ Still __ strove, _____ with his last ounce of

cour - age, _____ To reach _____ the un - reach - a - ble

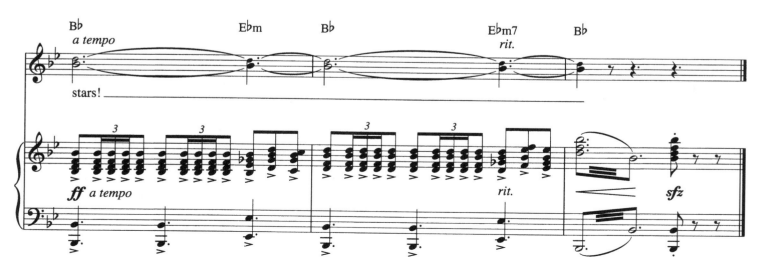

stars! _____

IT ONLY HAPPENS WHEN I DANCE WITH YOU

from the Motion Picture *Irving Berlin's Easter Parade*

Words and Music by
IRVING BERLIN

For the complete song see: HL00005101 *It Only Happens When I Dance with You* piano/vocal sheet music, and other sources.

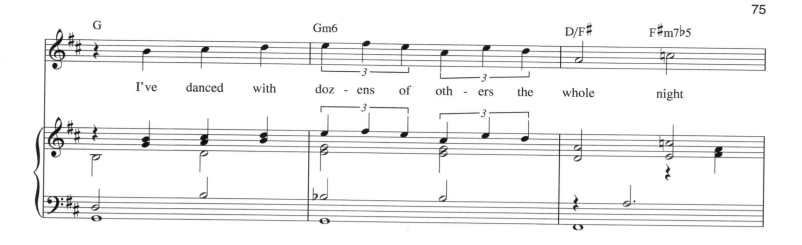

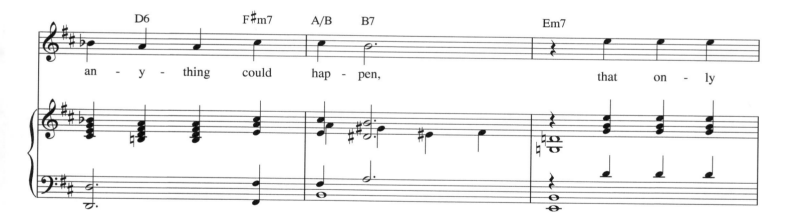

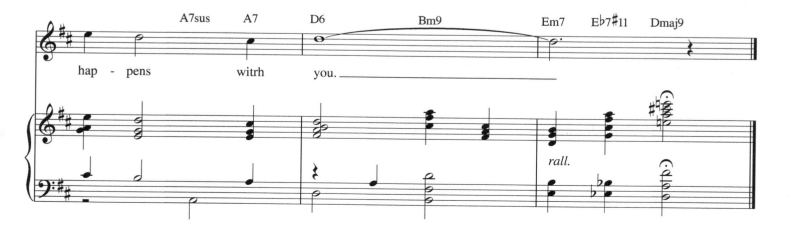

IT ONLY TAKES A MOMENT
from *Hello, Dolly!*

Music and Lyric by
JERRY HERMAN

For the complete song see: HL00383730 *Hello, Dolly!* vocal selections, and other sources.

JACKIE
(La chanson de Jacky)
from *Jacques Brel Is Alive and Well and Living in Paris*

Excerpt

French Words by JACQUES BREL
English Words by MORT SHUMAN and ERIC BLAU
Music by GERARD JOUANNEST

And tho' pink el - e - phants I'd see, though I'd be drunk as I could
be, still I would sing my song to me, a - bout the time they called me Jack - ie. If I could be for on - ly an
ho - ur, If I could be for an ho - ur ev - 'ry day, If I could be for just one lit - tle ho - ur, cute, cute,
cute, in a stu - pid ass way. _____

For the complete song see: HL00312047 *Jacques Brel Is Alive and Well and Living in Paris* vocal selections.

Excerpt

JAILHOUSE ROCK
from *Smokey Joe's Cafe*

Words and Music by JERRY LEIBER
and MIKE STOLLER

For the complete song see: HL00351489 *Jailhouse Rock* piano/vocal sheet music, and other sources.

Excerpt

JOEY, JOEY, JOEY
from *The Most Happy Fella*

By FRANK LOESSER

For the complete song see: HL00747033 *The Singer's Musical Theatre Anthology, Baritone/Bass Vol. 2,* and other sources.

Excerpt

KANSAS CITY
from *Oklahoma!*

Lyrics by OSCAR HAMMERSTEIN II
Music by RICHARD RODGERS

For the complete song see: HL01121041 *Oklahoma!* vocal selections, and other sources.

house is all com - plete._____ You c'n walk to priv - ies in the rain and

nev - er wet your feet! They've gone a - bout as fur as they c'n

go, _____ They've gone a - bout as fur as they c'n

go! _____

Excerpt

THE KITE
(Charlie Brown's Kite)
from *You're a Good Man, Charlie Brown*

Words and Music by
CLARK GESNER

For the complete song see: HL00740595 *You're A Good Man, Charlie Brown* vocal selections.

LIZZIE'S COMIN' HOME
from *110 in the Shade*

Words by TOM JONES
Music by HARVEY SCHMIDT

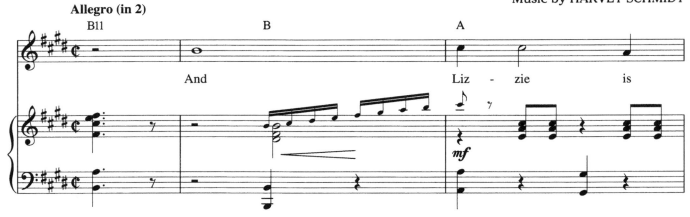

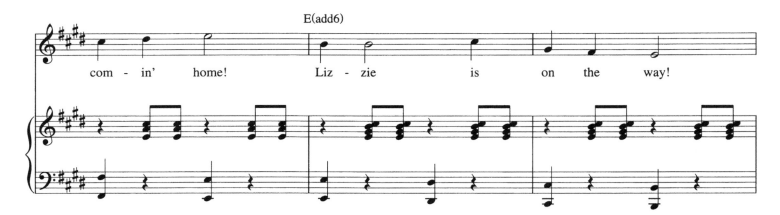

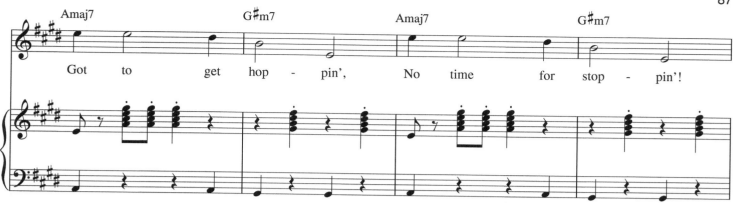

Got to get hop - pin', No time for stop - pin'!

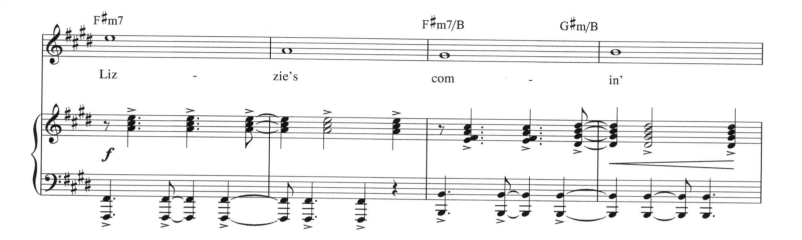

Liz - zie's com - in'

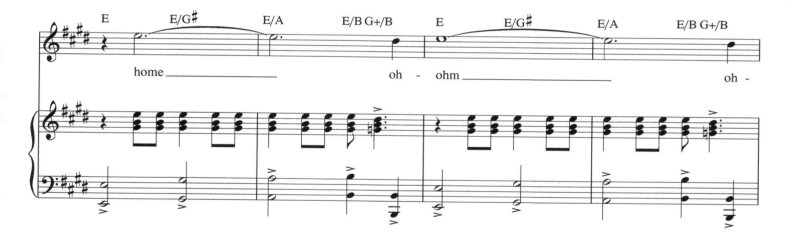

home _____ oh - ohm _____ oh -

ohm, _____ To - day!

Excerpt

LONELY ROOM
from *Oklahoma!*

Lyrics by OSCAR HAMMERSTEIN II
Music by RICHARD RODGERS

For the complete song see: HL00361074 *The Singer's Musical Theatre Anthology, Baritone/Bass Vol. 1 (Revised),* and other sources.

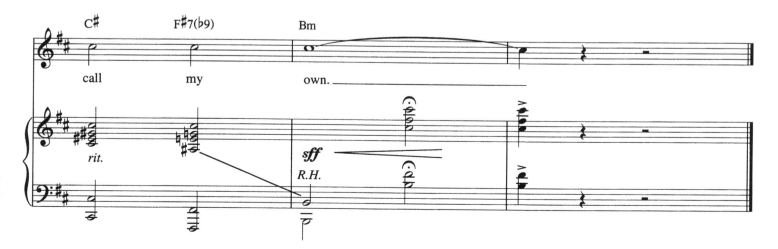

Excerpt

A LOT OF LIVIN' TO DO
from *Bye Bye Birdie*

Lyric by LEE ADAMS
Music by CHARLES STROUSE

For the complete song see: HL00313233 *Bye Bye Birdie* vocal selections, and other sources.

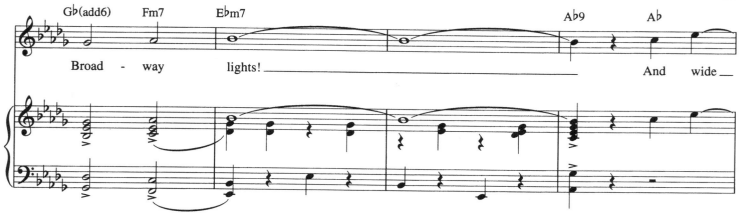

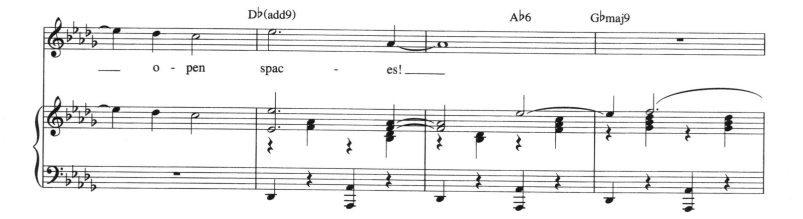

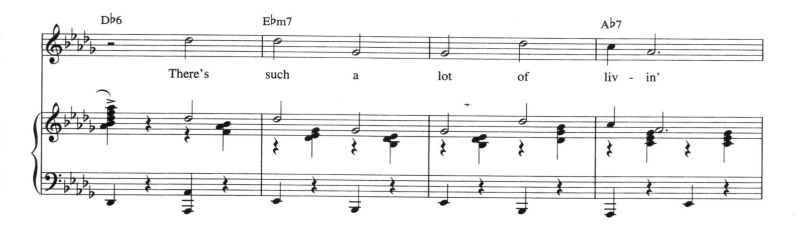

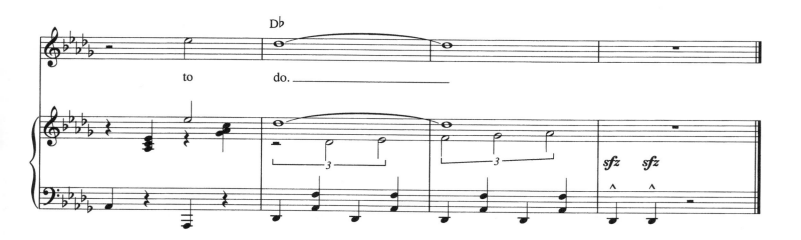

Excerpt

LOVE, I HEAR
from *A Funny Thing Happened on the Way to the Forum*

Words and Music by
STEPHEN SONDHEIM

Love, they say, _____ Makes you

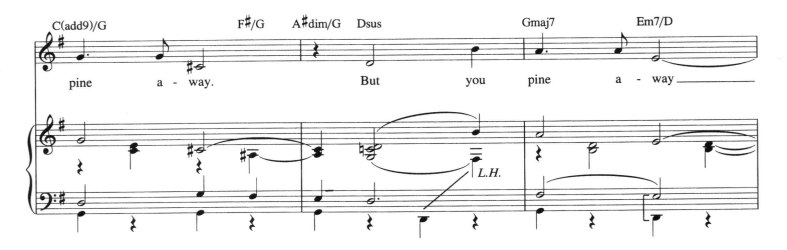

pine a - way. But you pine a - way _____

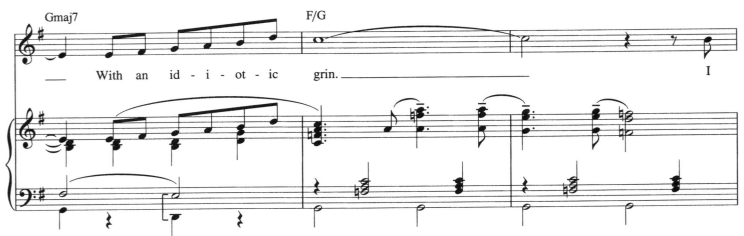

_____ With an id - i - ot - ic grin. _____ I

For the complete song see: HL00312151 *A Funny Thing Happened on the Way to the Forum* vocal selections, and other sources.

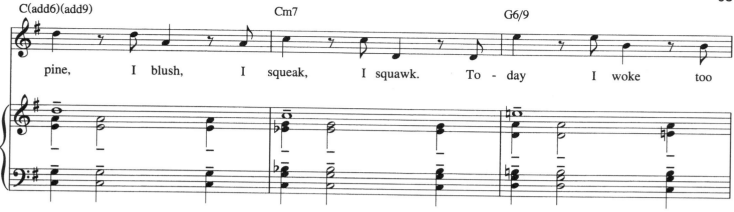

pine,   I blush,   I squeak,   I squawk.   To - day   I woke   too

weak   to walk.   What's love,   I hear,   I feel   I fear   I

know   I am,   I'm sure—   I mean,   I hope   I trust—   I pray—   I must—   Be

in! _____

Excerpt

LOVING YOU
from *Mame*

Music and Lyric by
JERRY HERMAN

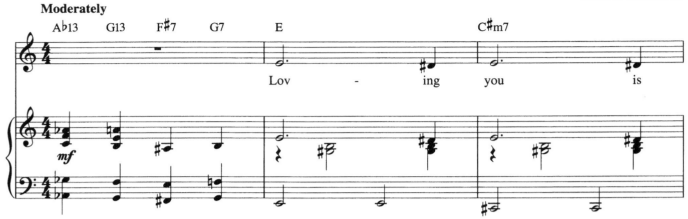

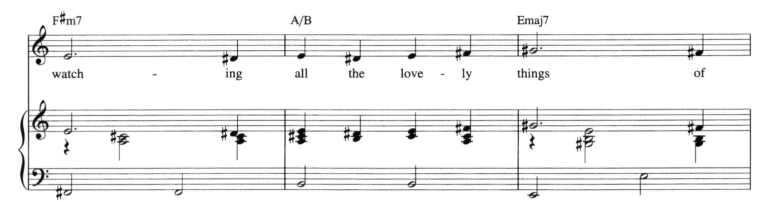

For the complete song see: HL00385217 *The Jerry Herman Songbook.*

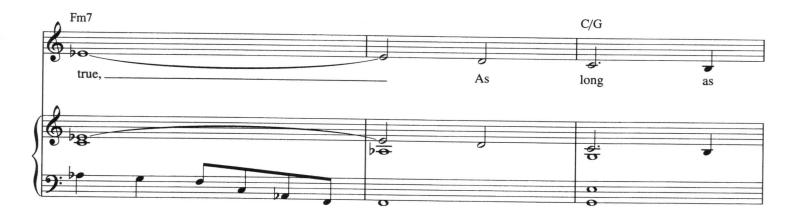

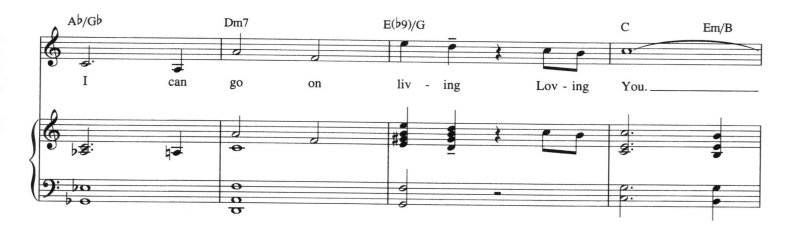

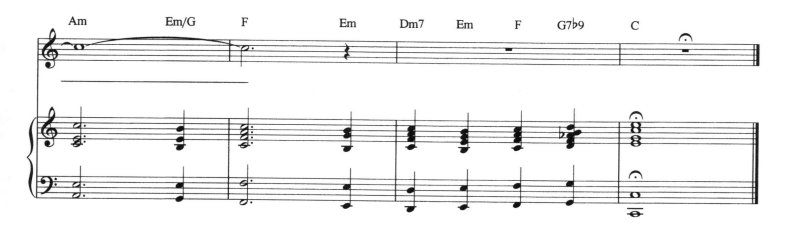

Excerpt

LUCK BE A LADY
from *Guys and Dolls*

By FRANK LOESSER

Brightly (in 2)

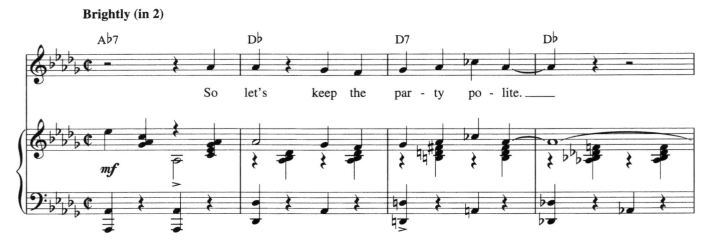

So let's keep the par-ty po-lite. ____

Nev-er get out of my sight. ____

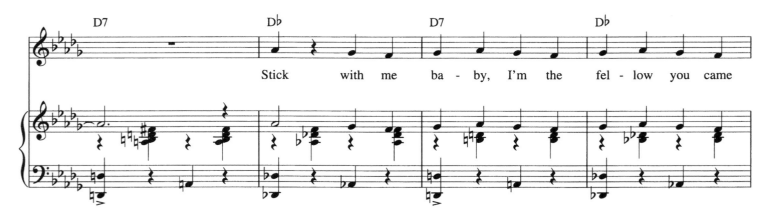

Stick with me ba-by, I'm the fel-low you came

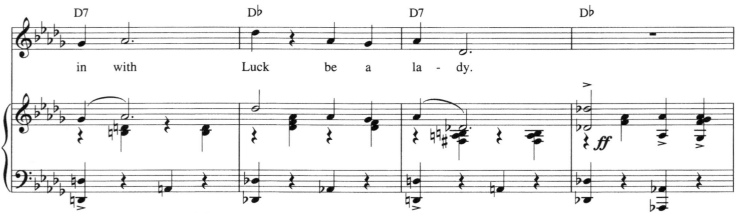

in with Luck be a la-dy.

For the complete song see: HL00747033 *The Singer's Musical Theatre Anthology, Baritone/Bass Vol. 2,* and other sources.

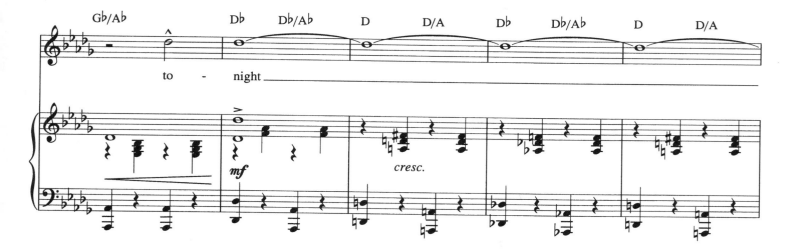

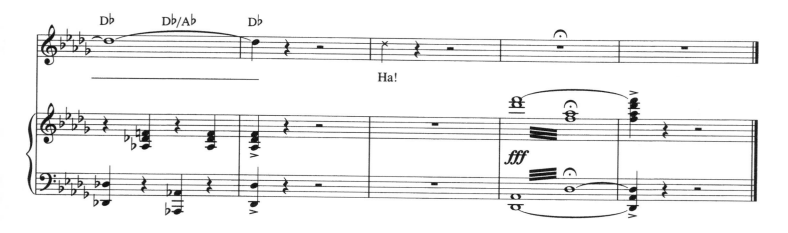

Excerpt

LET ME SING AND I'M HAPPY
from the Motion Picture *Mammy*

Words and Music by
IRVING BERLIN

Let me croon __ a low down blues __ to lift you out __ of your seat. If my song __ can reach your shoes __ and start you tap - ping your feet, I'm hap-py. Let me sing __ of Dix-ie's charms, __ the Swa-nee shore __ and moth-er's arms. __ And if my song __ can make you home - sick, I'm hap - py.

For the complete song see: HL00005137 *Let Me Sing and I'm Happy* piano/vocal sheet music, and other sources.

Excerpt

MY DEFENSES ARE DOWN
from the Stage Production *Annie Get Your Gun*

Words and Music by
IRVING BERLIN

For the complete song see: HL00747033 *The Singer's Musical Theatre Anthology, Baritone/Bass Vol. 2,* and other sources.

MAKE SOMEONE HAPPY
from *Do Re Mi*

Words by BETTY COMDEN
and ADOLPH GREEN
Music by JULE STYNE

For the complete song see: HL00361073 *The Singer's Musical Theatre Anthology, Tenor Vol. 1,* and other sources.

found her, Build your world a - round her.

Make some - one hap - py, Make just one

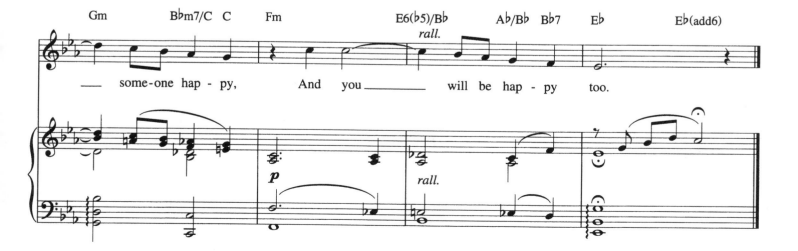

some-one hap - py, And you will be hap - py too.

MAN OF LA MANCHA
(I, Don Quixote)
from *Man of La Mancha*

Lyric by JOE DARION
Music by MITCH LEIGH

Tempo Paso Doble

For the complete song see: HL00361074 *The Singer's Musical Theatre Anthology, Baritone/Bass Vol. 1 (Revised)*, and other sources.

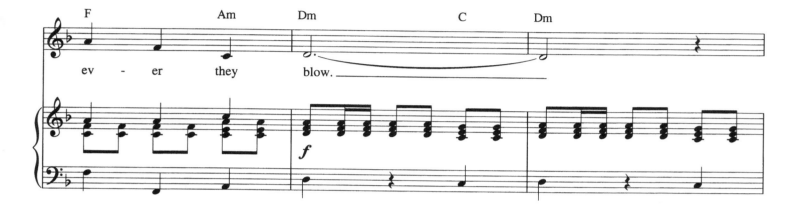

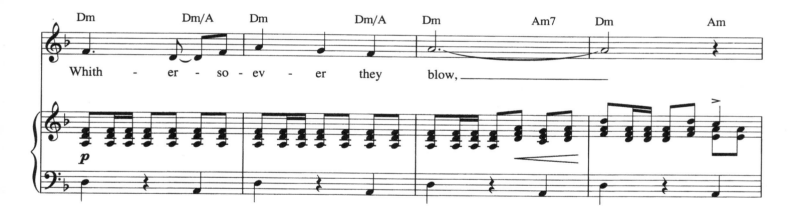

Excerpt

ME
from Walt Disney's *Beauty and the Beast: The Broadway Musical*

Music by ALAN MENKEN
Lyrics by TIM RICE

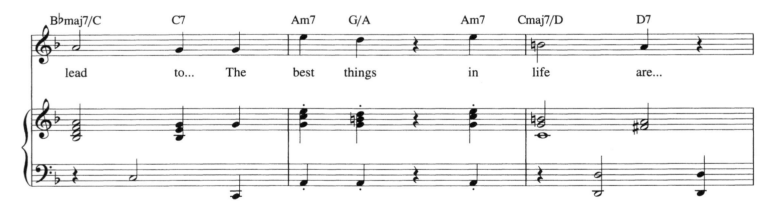

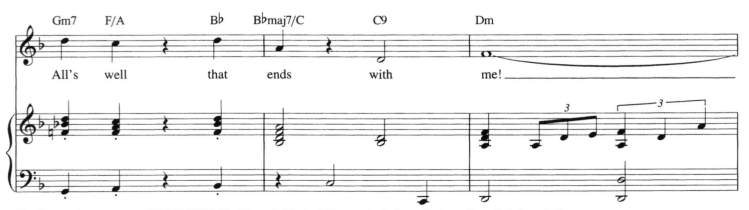

For the complete song see: HL00740125 *The Singer's Musical Theatre Anthology, Baritone/Bass Vol. 3*, and other sources.

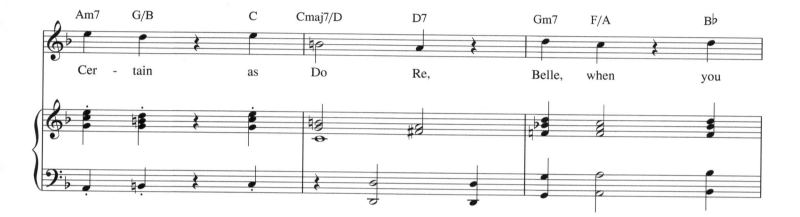

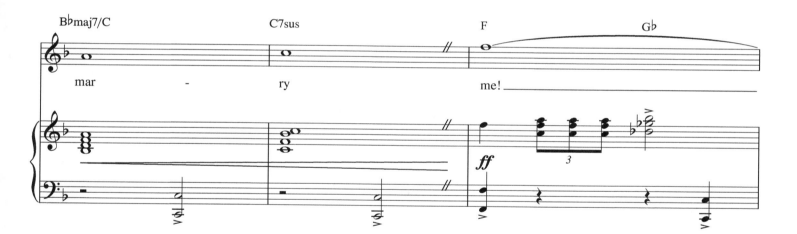

Excerpt

MY NAME
from the Columbia Pictures-Romulus Film *Oliver!*

Words and Music by
LIONEL BART

For the complete song see: HL00747033 *The Singer's Musical Theatre Anthology, Baritone/Bass Vol. 2*, and other sources.

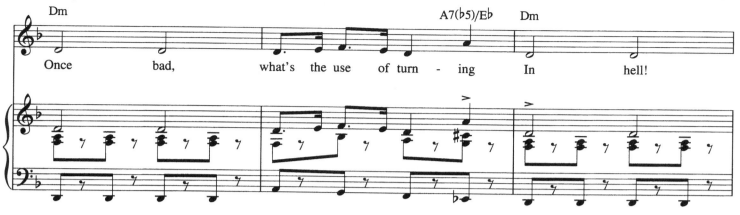

Excerpt

MY ROMANCE
from *Jumbo*

Words by LORENZ HART
Music by RICHARD RODGERS

For the complete song see: HL00313093 *Jumbo* vocal selections, and other sources.

Excerpt

OLD DEVIL MOON
from *Finian's Rainbow*

Words by E.Y. HARBURG
Music by BURTON LANE

Andante con moto

For the complete song see: HL00312138 *Finian's Rainbow* vocal selections, and other sources.

NOTHING CAN STOP ME NOW!

Excerpt

from *The Roar of the Greasepaint - The Smell of the Crowd*

Words and Music by ANTHONY NEWLEY
and LESLIE BRICUSSE

For the complete song see: HL00311521 *Broadway Musicals Show by Show 1960-1971*, and other sources.

who can say?____ But I know I

will some day.____ Watch out, world, I'm

on my way,___ And I'll suc-ceed___ some-how._____

__ Noth-ing can stop___ me now._____

Excerpt

ON A CLEAR DAY
(You Can See Forever)
from *On A Clear Day You Can See Forever*

Words by ALAN JAY LERNER
Music by BURTON LANE

For the complete song see: HL00740125 *The Singer's Musical Theatre Anthology, Baritone/Bass Vol. 3*, and other sources.

Excerpt

ON BROADWAY
from *Smokey Joe's Cafe*

Words and Music by BARRY MANN, CYNTHIA WEIL,
MIKE STOLLER and JERRY LEIBER

Moderately, with a beat

They say that I won't last too long on Broad-way.

I'll catch a Grey-hound bus for home they say.

But they're dead wrong, I know they are, 'cause I can play this here gui-tar

and I won't quit till I'm a star on Broad-way.

For the complete song see: HL00353367 *On Broadway* piano/vocal sheet music, and other sources.

ON THE STREET WHERE YOU LIVE

Excerpt

from *My Fair Lady*

Words by ALAN JAY LERNER
Music by FREDERICK LOEWE

For the complete song see: HL00312265 *My Fair Lady* vocal selections, and other sources.

Excerpt

ONCE IN A LIFETIME

from the Musical Production *Stop the World – I Want to Get Off*

Words and Music by LESLIE BRICUSSE
and ANTHONY NEWLEY

For the complete song see: HL00315332 *Theatre Songs for Singers,* and other sources.

Excerpt

ONCE IN LOVE WITH AMY
from *Where's Charley?*

By FRANK LOESSER

For the complete song see: HL00747033 *The Singer's Musical Theatre Anthology, Baritone/Bass Vol. 2,* and other sources.

once in love with A - my, ___ Al - ways in love with

A - my, ___ Ev - er and ev - er sweet - ly you'll ro-mance 'er.

Trou - ble is the an - swer will be _____ That A - my'd rath - er stay in

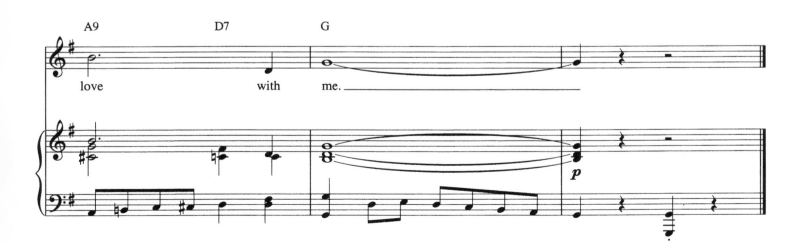

love with me. _____

ONCE UPON A TIME
from the Broadway Musical *All American*

Lyric by LEE ADAMS
Music by CHARLES STROUSE

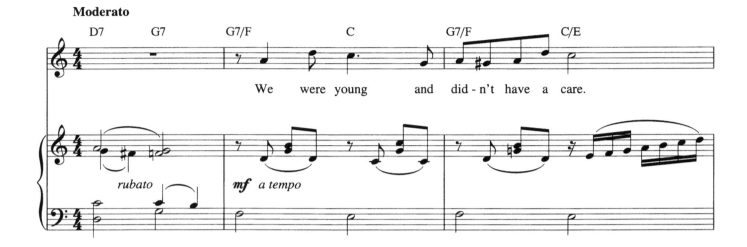

For the complete song see: HL00313247 *The Songs of Charles Strouse,* and other sources.

Ev - 'ry - thing was ours, _____ How hap - py we were then; _____

___ But some - how once up - on a time _____ nev - er comes a -

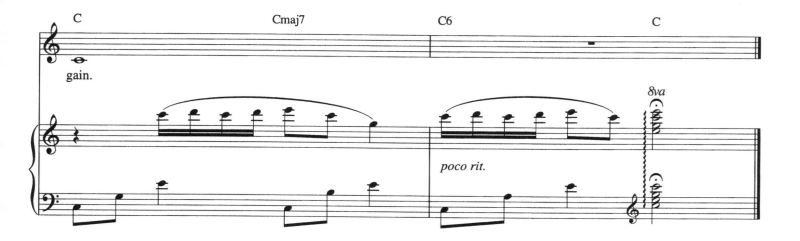

gain.

OUT OF THIS WORLD
from the Motion Picture *Out of This World*

Lyric by JOHNNY MERCER
Music by HAROLD ARLEN

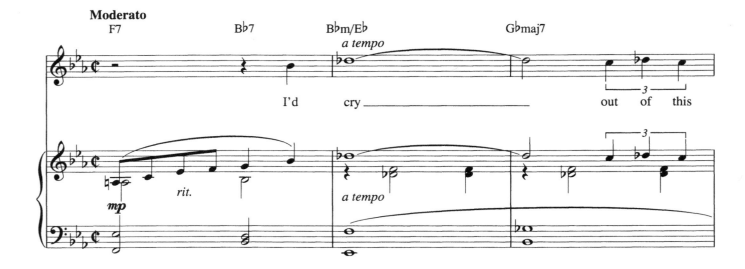

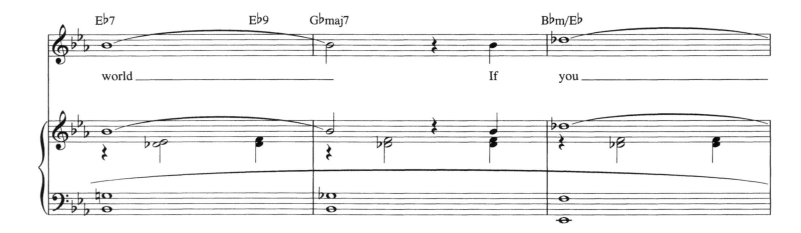

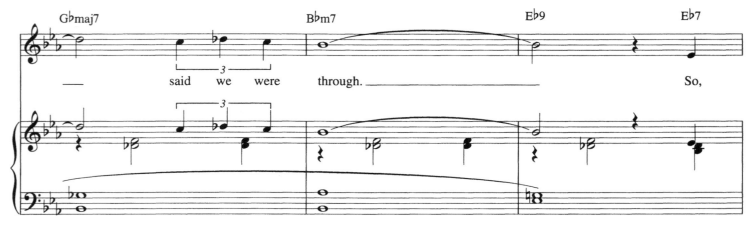

For the complete song see: HL00359080 *The Harold Arlen Songbook,* and other sources.

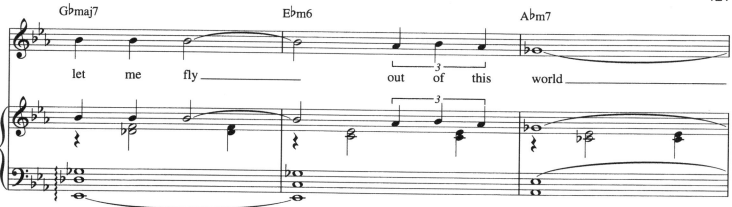

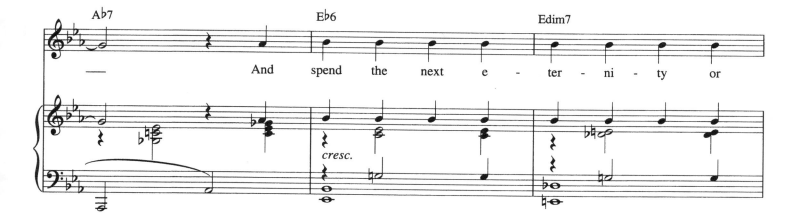

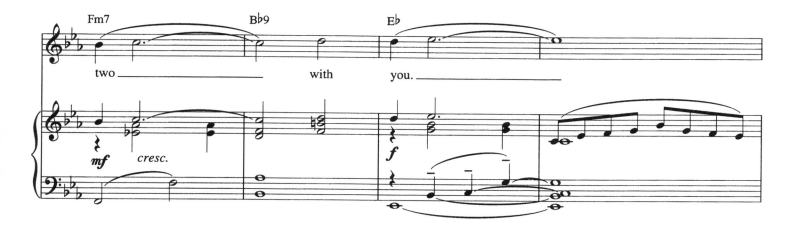

Excerpt

OUT THERE
from Walt Disney's *The Hunchback of Notre Dame*

Music by ALAN MENKEN
Lyrics by STEPHEN SCHWARTZ

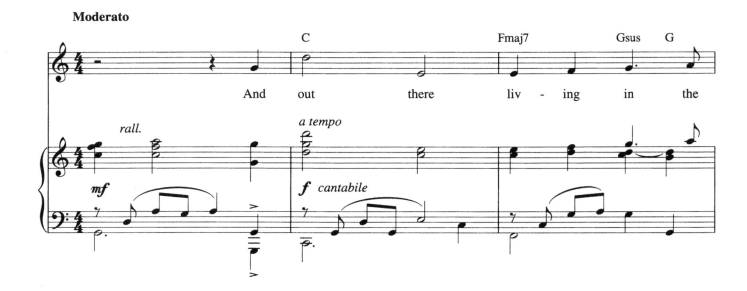

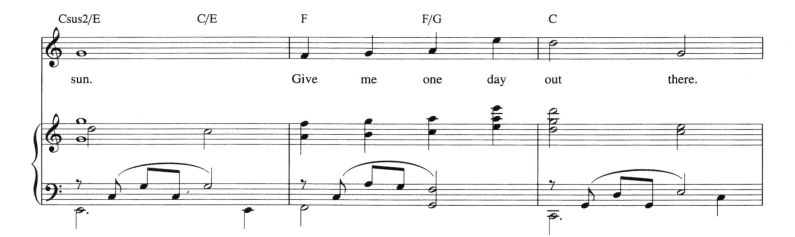

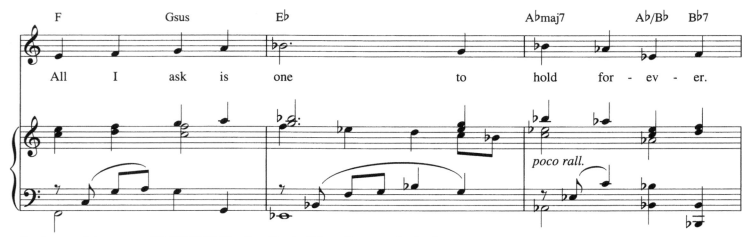

For the complete song see: HL00313045 *The Hunchback of Notre Dame* vocal selections.

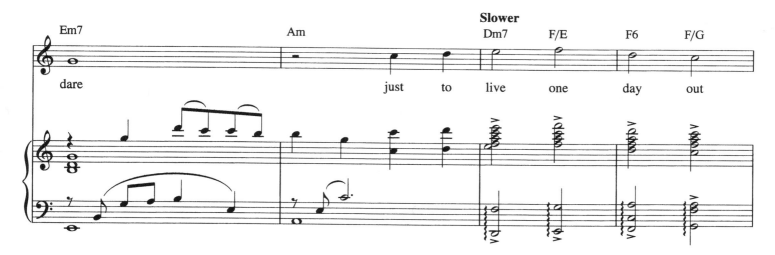

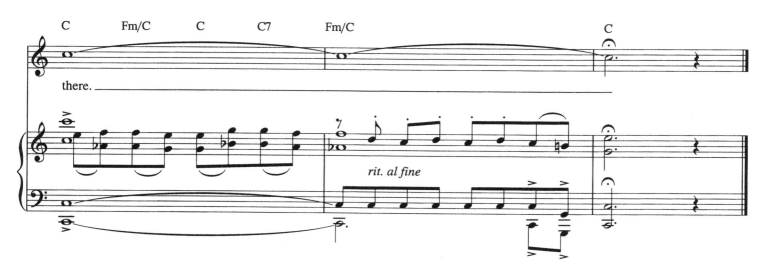

PEOPLE WILL SAY WE'RE IN LOVE

Excerpt

from *Oklahoma!*

Lyrics by OSCAR HAMMERSTEIN II
Music by RICHARD RODGERS

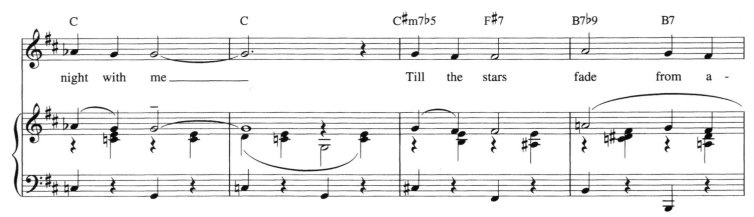

For the complete song see: HL00304847 *People Will Say We're in Love* piano/vocal sheet music, and other sources.

Excerpt

PUT ON A HAPPY FACE
from *Bye, Bye, Birdie*

Lyric by LEE ADAMS
Music by CHARLES STROUSE

For the complete song see: HL00312233 *Bye, Bye, Birdie* vocal selections, and other sources.

Excerpt

THE SADDER BUT WISER GIRL

from Meredith Willson's *The Music Man*

By MEREDITH WILLSON

Moderate 2

I flinch, I shy, when the

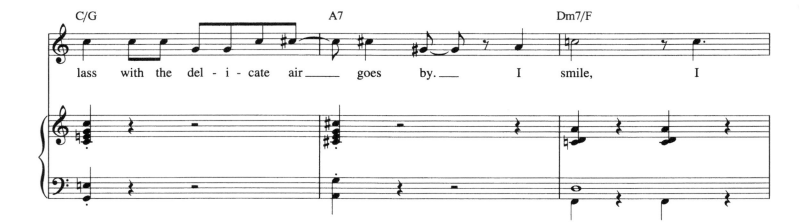

lass with the del - i - cate air ___ goes by. ___ I smile, I

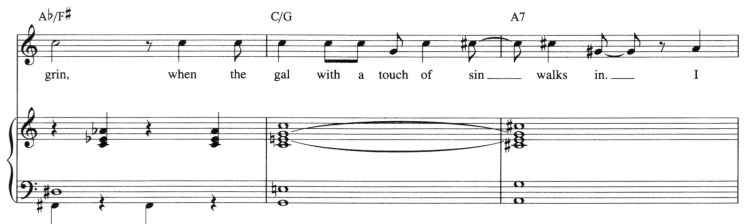

grin, when the gal with a touch of sin ___ walks in. ___ I

For the complete song see: HL00740125 *The Singer's Musical Theatre Anthology, Baritone/Bass Vol. 3.*

hope, I pray, for Hes - ter to win just

one more "A." __ The sad - der but wis - er girl's the

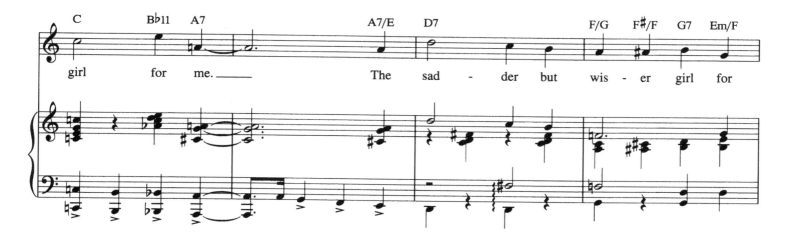

girl for me. ___ The sad - der but wis - er girl for

me. ___

Excerpt

SANTA FE
from Walt Disney's *Newsies*

Lyrics by JACK FELDMAN
Music by ALAN MENKEN

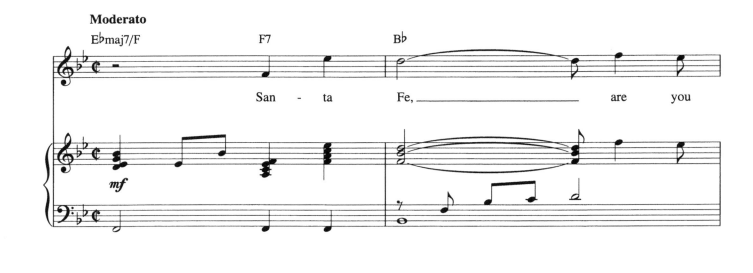

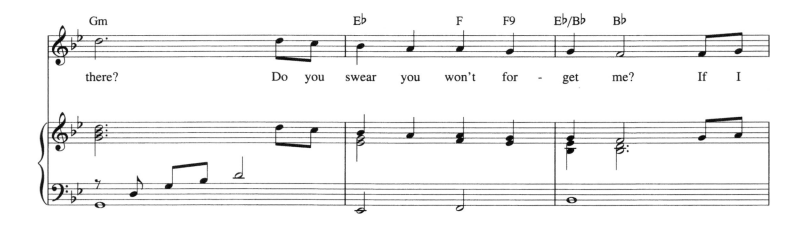

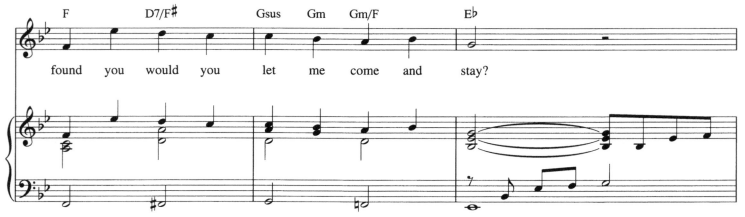

For the complete song see: HL00740125 *The Singer's Musical Theatre Anthology, Baritone/Bass Vol. 3,* and other sources.

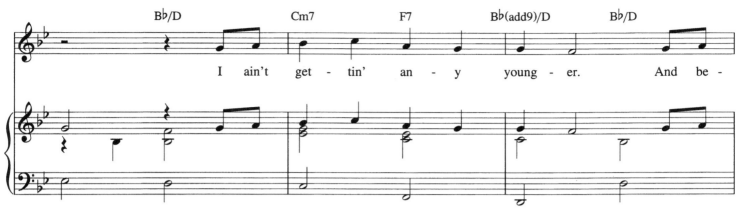

I ain't get - tin' an - y young - er. And be -

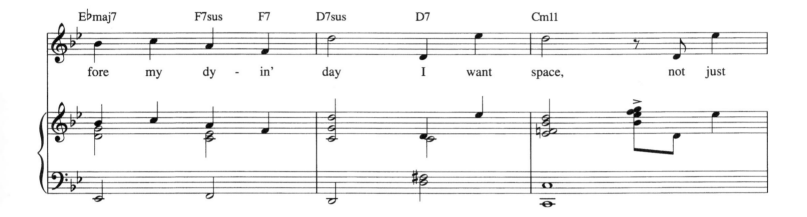

fore my dy - in' day I want space, not just

air. Let 'em laugh in my face, I don't care. Save a

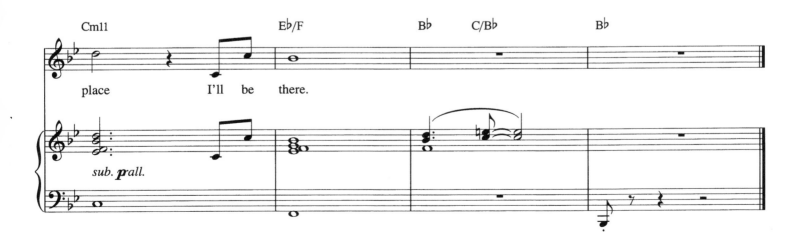

place I'll be there.

A SECRETARY IS NOT A TOY

from *How to Succeed in Business Without Really Trying*

By FRANK LOESSER

Moderato (Broadly)

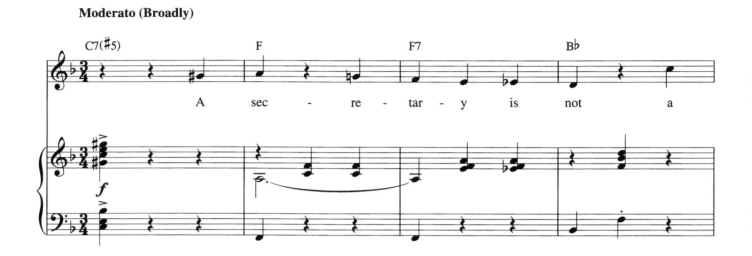

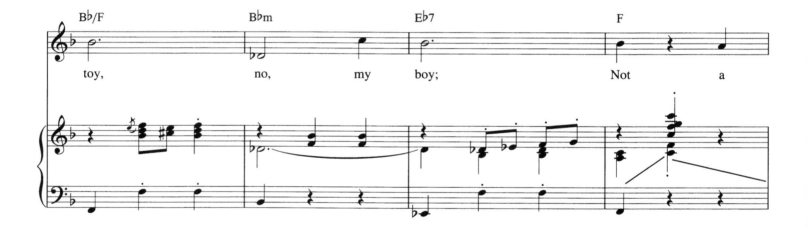

For the complete song see: HL00444442 *The Frank Loesser Songbook.*

han - dle in search of some pu - er - ile joy.

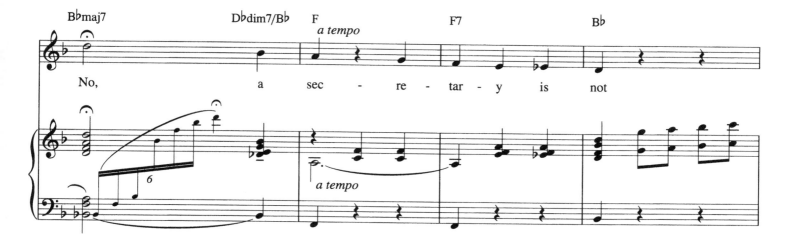

No, a sec - re - tar - y is not

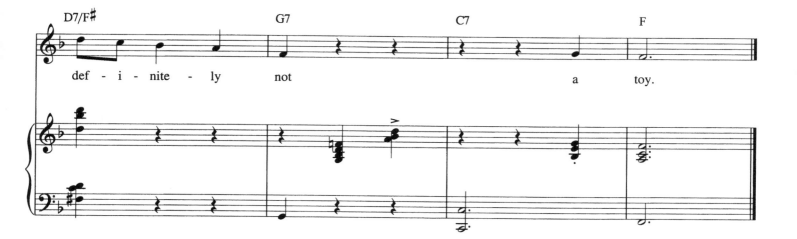

def - i - nite - ly not a toy.

Excerpt

SHE TOUCHED ME
from *Drat! The Cat!*

Lyric by IRA LEVIN
Music by MILTON SCHAFER

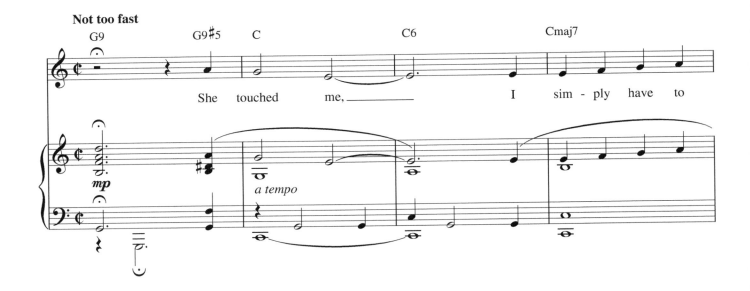

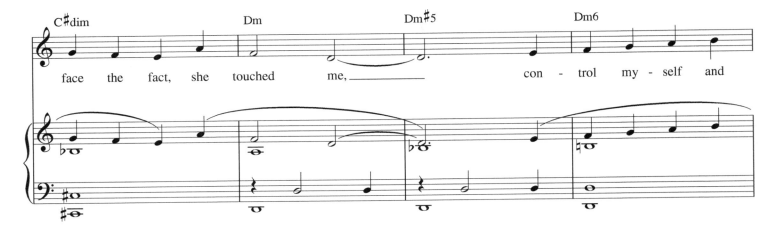

For the complete song see: HL00359570 *The Definitive Broadway Collection,* and other sources.

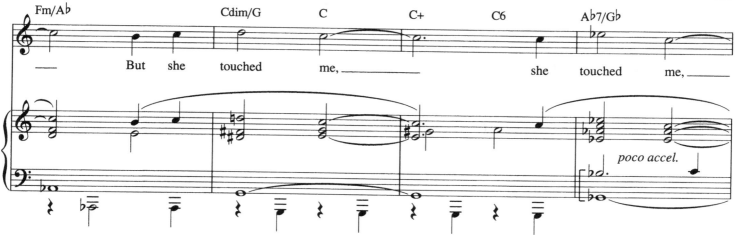

But she touched me, _____ she touched me, _____

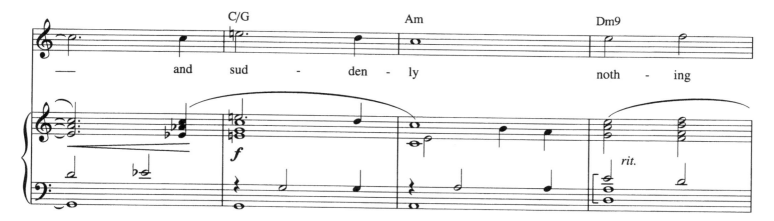

and sud - den - ly noth - ing

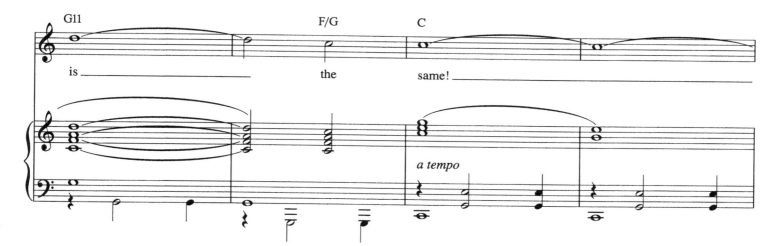

is _____ the same! _____

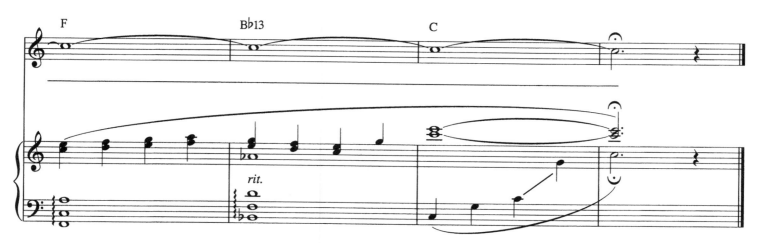

THE SHORTEST DAY OF THE YEAR

Excerpt

from *The Boys from Syracuse*

Words by LORENZ HART
Music by RICHARD RODGERS

For the complete song see: HL00312045 *The Boys from Syracuse* vocal selections, and other sources.

Excerpt

SOME ENCHANTED EVENING
from *South Pacific*

Lyrics by OSCAR HAMMERSTEIN II
Music by RICHARD RODGERS

Slowly, with expression

For the complete song see: HL00361074 *The Singer's Musical Theatre Anthology, Baritone/Bass Vol. 1 (Revised)*, and other sources.

SOMEBODY LOVES ME
from *George White's Scandals of 1924*

Excerpt

Words by B.G. DeSYLVA
and BALLARD MacDONALD
Music by GEORGE GERSHWIN
French Version by EMELIA RENAUD

Allegro moderato

For ev - 'ry girl who pass - es me I shout, hey!

may - be, you were meant to be my lov - ing

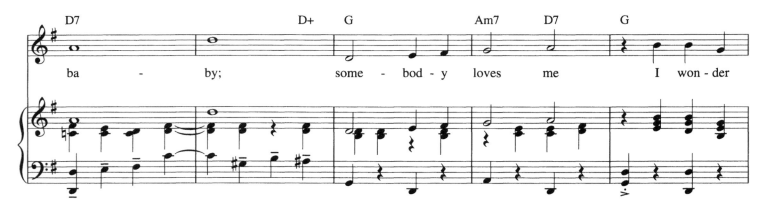

ba - by; some - bod - y loves me I won - der

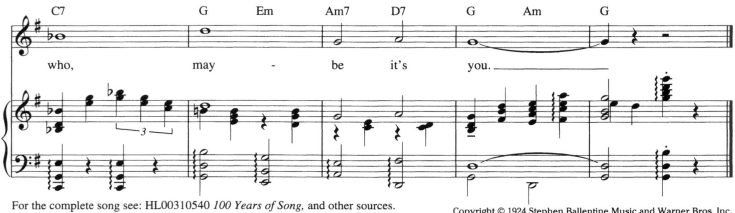

who, may - be it's you.

For the complete song see: HL00310540 *100 Years of Song*, and other sources.

Excerpt

SOMEONE LIKE YOU

from *Do I Hear a Waltz?*

Music by RICHARD RODGERS
Lyrics by STEPHEN SONDHEIM

Moderately slow

Sud-den-ly the door Won-der-ful sur-prise! Won-der-ful and more. Be-fore our eyes. _____ We thought that _____ sur-pris - es Were o - ver for - ev - er And then came some-one like you. _____

For the complete song see: HL00312115 *Do I Hear a Waltz?* vocal selections.

Excerpt

SOMETHING, SOMEWHERE

from *Two By Two*

Lyrics by MARTIN CHARNIN
Music by RICHARD RODGERS

Allegro agitato (in 1)

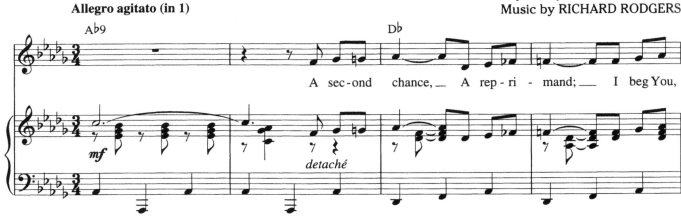

A sec-ond chance, __ A rep-ri-mand; __ I beg You,

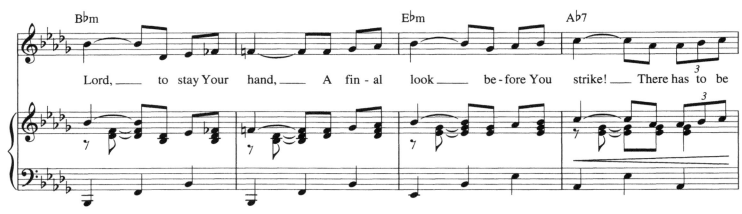

Lord, __ to stay Your hand, __ A fin-al look __ be-fore You strike! __ There has to be

some-thing, some-where, some-thing, some-where, some-where,

some-thing that You like! __

For the complete song see: HL00312460 *Two By Two* vocal selections.

Excerpt

SOMETHING WAS MISSING
from the Musical Production *Annie*

Lyric by MARTIN CHARNIN
Music by CHARLES STROUSE

For the complete song see: HL00383056*Annie* vocal selections.

Excerpt

STAYIN' ALIVE
from the Broadway Musical *Saturday Night Fever*

Words and Music by ROBIN GIBB,
MAURICE GIBB and BARRY GIBB

For the complete song see: HL00313160 *Saturday Night Fever* vocal selections, and other sources.

Excerpt

STEPPIN' OUT WITH MY BABY
from the Motion Picture *Irving Berlin's Easter Parade*

Words and Music by
IRVING BERLIN

Medium jump tempo

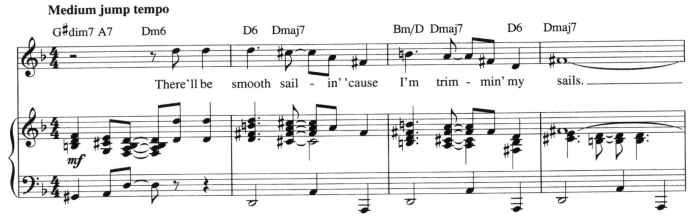

There'll be smooth sail - in' 'cause I'm trim - min' my sails.

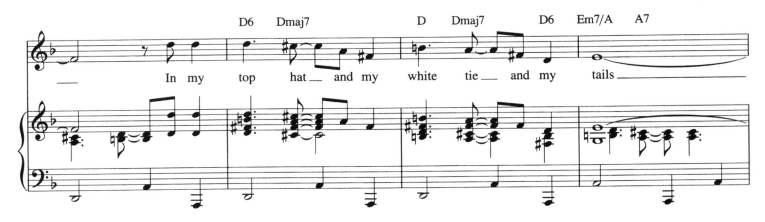

In my top hat __ and my white tie __ and my tails __

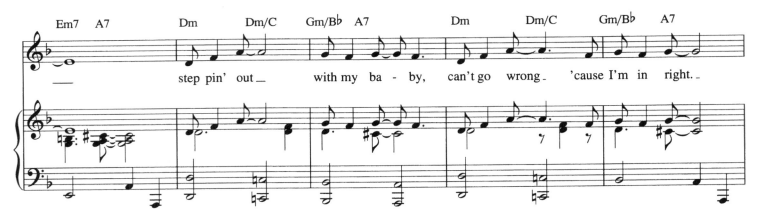

step pin' out __ with my ba - by, can't go wrong __ 'cause I'm in right.

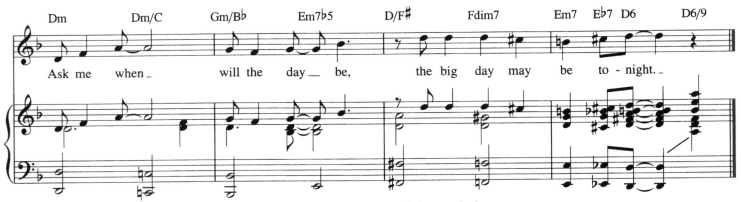

Ask me when __ will the day __ be, the big day may be to - night. __

For the complete song see: HL00005206 *Steppin' Out with My Baby*, piano/vocal sheet, and other sources.

Excerpt

THAT'S FOR ME
from *State Fair*

Lyrics by OSCAR HAMMERSTEIN II
Music by RICHARD RODGERS

Slowly, with expression

I left you stand-ing un-der stars, The day's ad-ven-tures are through ___ There's noth-ing for me but the dream in my heart and the dream in my heart, That's for you! ___ Oh my dar-ling, That's for you! ___

For the complete song see: HL00312043 *State Fair* vocal selections, and other sources.

Excerpt

TEN MINUTES AGO

from *Cinderella*

Lyrics by OSCAR HAMMERSTEIN II
Music by RICHARD RODGERS

Tempo di Valse (in 1)

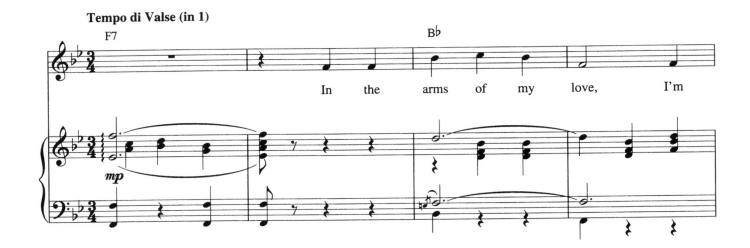

In the arms of my love, I'm

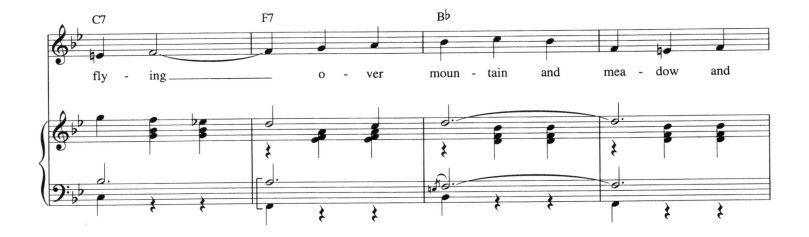

fly - ing _____ o - ver moun - tain and mea - dow and

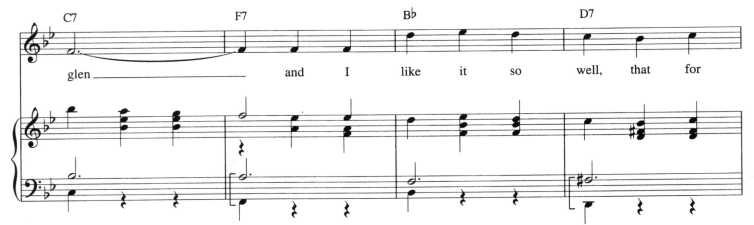

glen _____ and I like it so well, that for

For the complete song see: HL00361074 *The Singer's Musical Theatre Anthology, Baritone/Bass Vol. 1 (Revised),* and other sources.

all I can tell, I may nev - er come

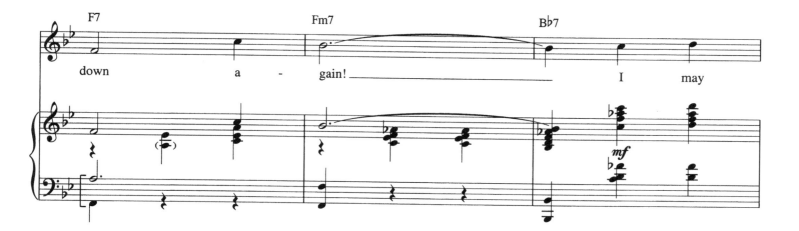

down a - gain! I may

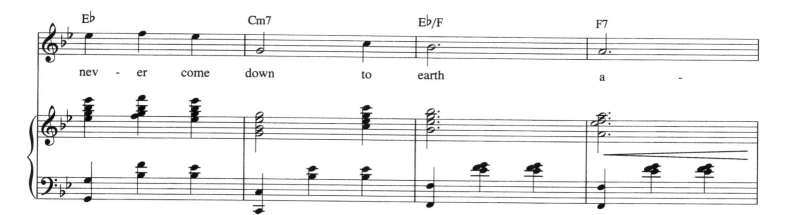

nev - er come down to earth a -

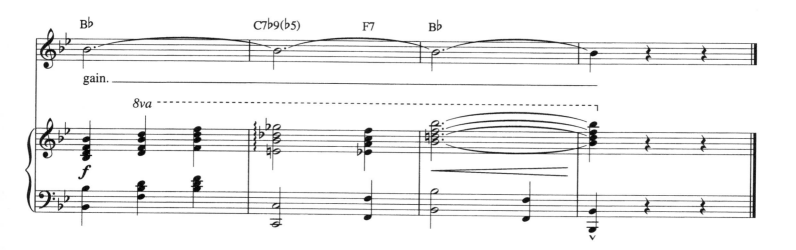

gain.

Excerpt

THEY CALL THE WIND MARIA

from *Paint Your Wagon*

Words by ALAN JAY LERNER
Music by FREDERICK LOEWE

For the complete song see: HL00361074 *The Singer's Musical Theatre Anthology, Baritone/Bass Vol. 1 (Revised)*, and other sources.

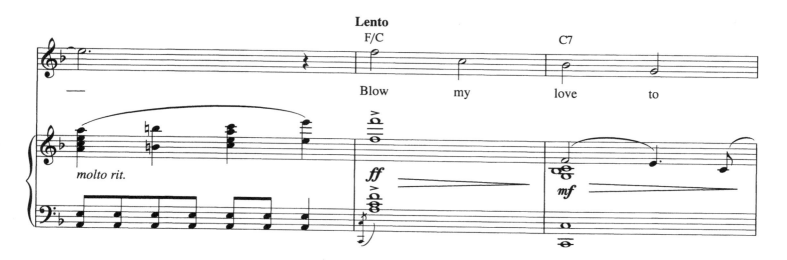

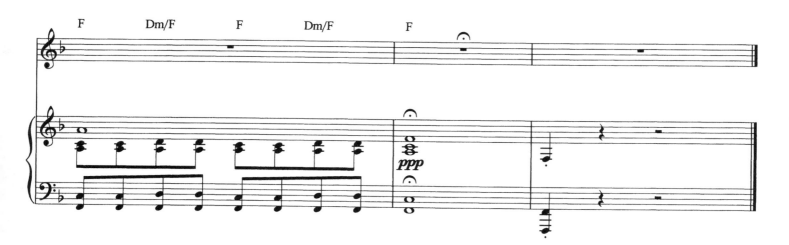

Excerpt

'TIL HIM
from *The Producers*

Music and Lyrics by
MEL BROOKS

Moderato (ballad-like)

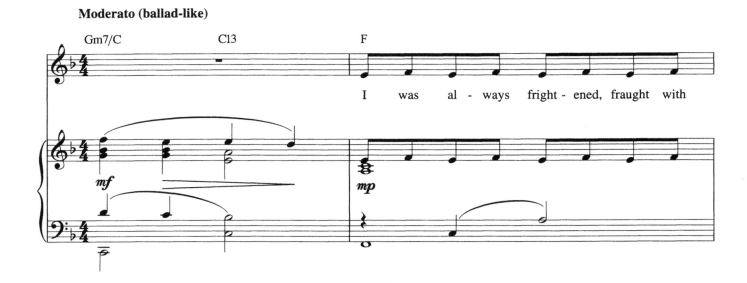

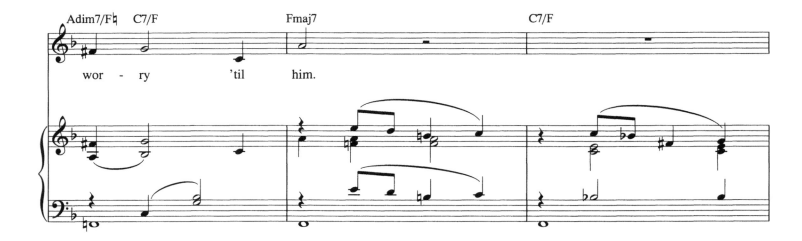

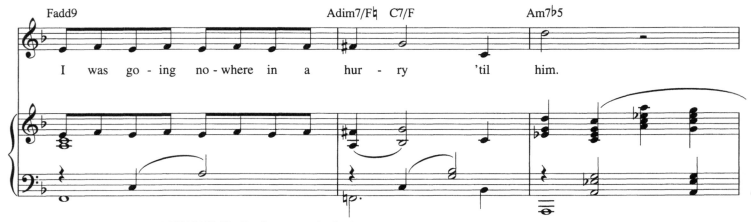

For the complete song see: HL00313189 *The Producers* vocal selections.

He filled up my emp - ty life,

filled it to the brim. There could nev - er ev - er be an -

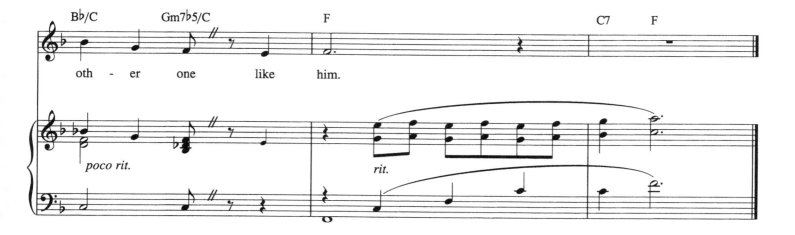

oth - er one like him.

THERE'S NO REASON IN THE WORLD

Excerpt

from *Milk and Honey*

Music and Lyric by
JERRY HERMAN

For the complete song see: HL00384251 *Milk and Honey* vocal selections, and other sources.

Excerpt # WITH SO LITTLE TO BE SURE OF

from *Anyone Can Whistle*

Words and Music by
STEPHEN SONDHEIM

Moderato, with expression

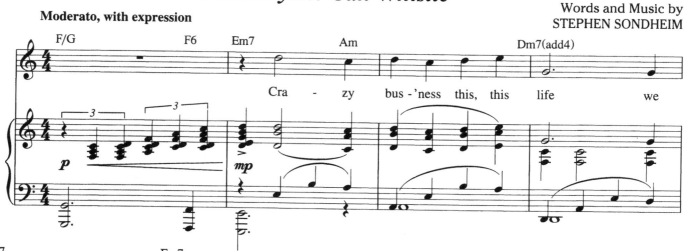

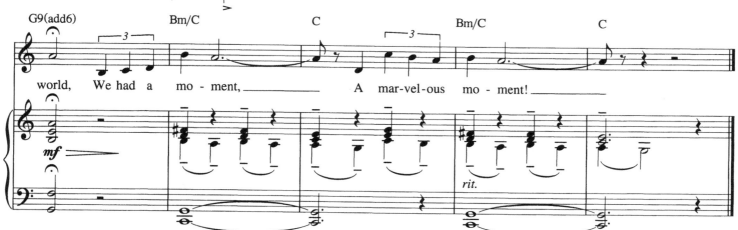

For the complete song see: HL00312010 *Anyone Can Whistle* vocal selections, and other sources.

WERE THINE THAT SPECIAL FACE

Excerpt

from *Kiss Me, Kate*

Words and Music by
COLE PORTER

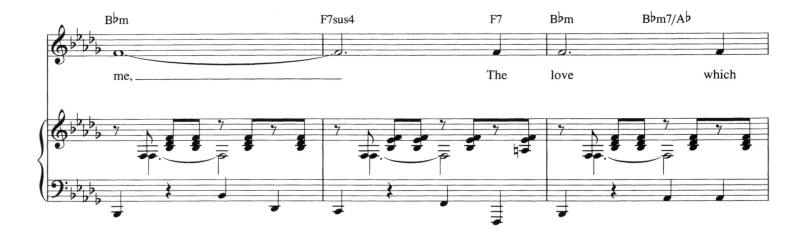

For the complete song see: HL00361074 *The Singer's Musical Theatre Anthology, Baritone/Bass Vol. 1 (Revised)*, and other sources.

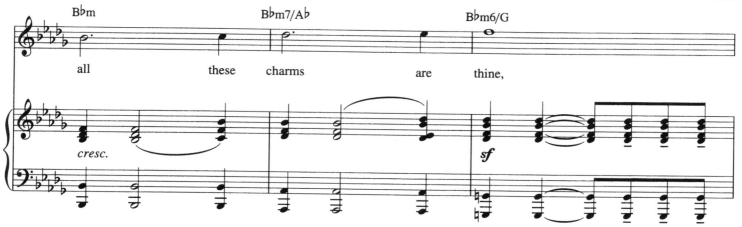

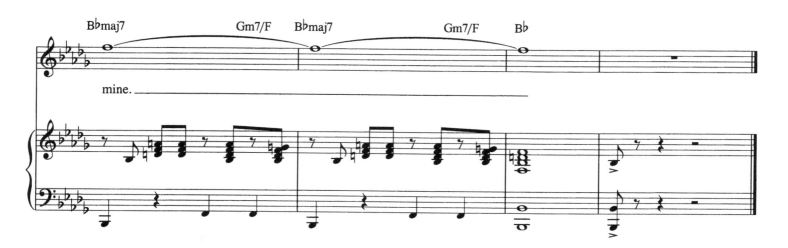

WHAT KIND OF FOOL AM I?

from *Stop the World - I Want to Get Off*

Words and Music by ANTHONY NEWLEY
and LESLIE BRICUSSE

Moderately slow

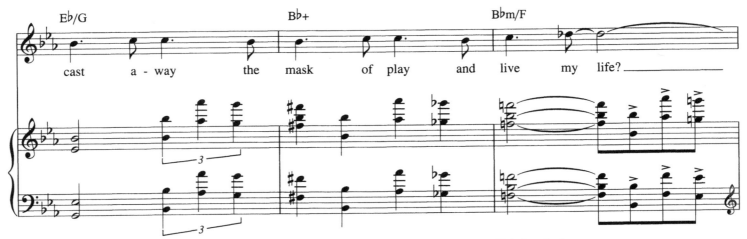

For the complete song see: HL00740125 *The Singer's Musical Theatre Anthology, Baritone/Bass Vol. 3*, and other sources.

Why can't I fall in love 'til I don't

give a damn? And may-be then I'll know what

kind of fool I am.

WHEN SHE LOVED ME
from Walt Disney's *Toy Story 2 - A Pixar Film*

Music and Lyrics by
RANDY NEWMAN

For the complete song see: HL00313152 *Toy Story 2* piano/vocal/guitar songbook, and other sources.

she loved me. Through the sum-mer and the fall, we

had each oth - er, that was all. Just she and I to - geth - er, like

it was meant to be. And when she was lone - ly, I was there to com - fort her, and I

knew _____ that she loved me.

Excerpt

WHERE IS THE LIFE THAT LATE I LED?

from *Kiss Me, Kate*

Words and Music by
COLE PORTER

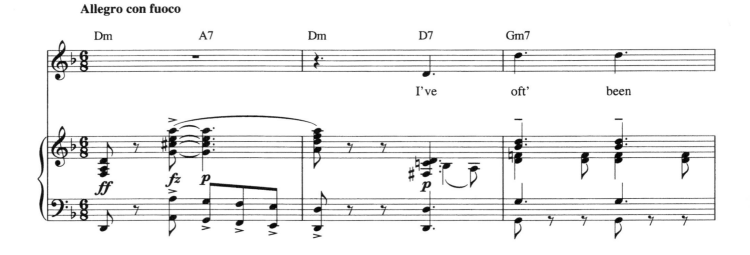

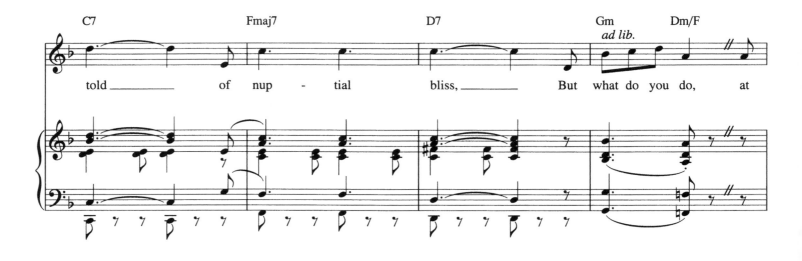

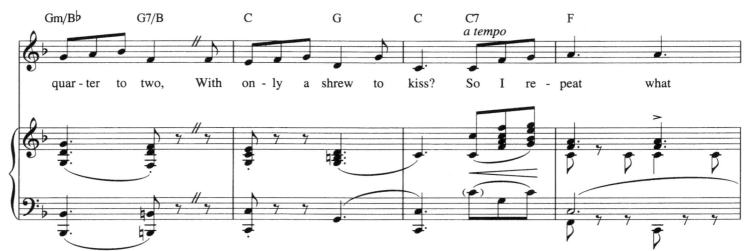

For the complete song see: HL00361074 *The Singer's Musical Theatre Anthology, Baritone/Bass Vol. 1 (Revised)*, and other sources.

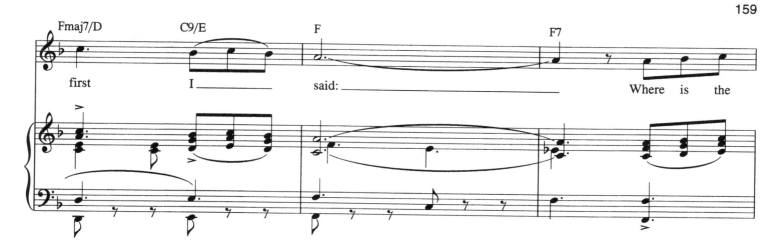

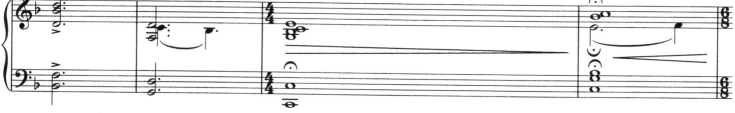

Excerpt

WHERE OR WHEN
from *Babes in Arms*

Words by LORENZ HART
Music by RICHARD RODGERS

For the complete song see: HL00740167 *The Songs of Richard Rodgers - Low Voice,* and other sources.

And so it seems that we have met be -

fore, and laughed be - fore, and

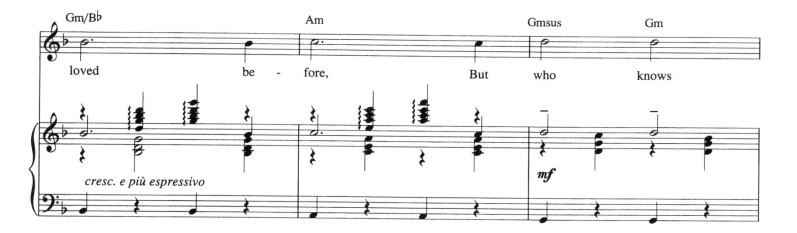

loved be - fore, But who knows

where or when! _____

Excerpt

WHO CAN I TURN TO?
(When Nobody Needs Me)
from *The Roar of the Greasepaint - The Smell of the Crowd*

Words and Music by LESLIE BRICUSSE
and ANTHONY NEWLEY

For the complete song see: HL00313156 *The Roar of the Greasepaint - The Smell of the Crowd* vocal selections, and other sources.

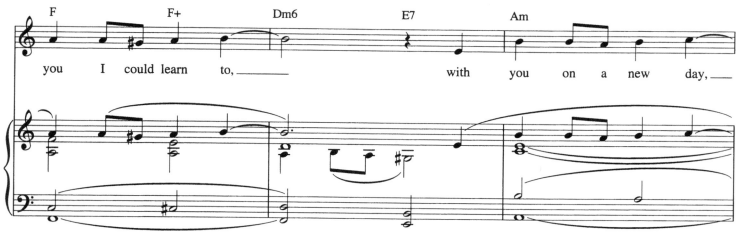

you I could learn to, _____ with you on a new day, _____

_____ But who can I turn to if you turn a-

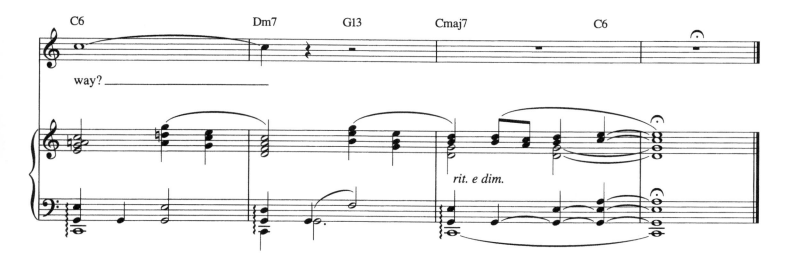

way? _____

Excerpt

WHO DO YOU LOVE I HOPE
from *Annie Get Your Gun*

Words and Music by
IRVING BERLIN

Moderato, with a lift

Is it the bak - er who gave you a cake?_ I saw that look_ in his eye_ Is it the butch - er who brought you a steak?_ Say that it is_ and I'll die._

For the complete song see: HL00005263 *Who Do You Love I Hope* piano/vocal sheet.

Who do you love __ I hope?

Who would you kiss __ I hope? Who is it go - ing to

be? _____ I hope, I hope, I hope it's me. ___

Excerpt

WHY SHOULD I WAKE UP?
from the Musical *Cabaret*

Words by FRED EBB
Music by JOHN KANDER

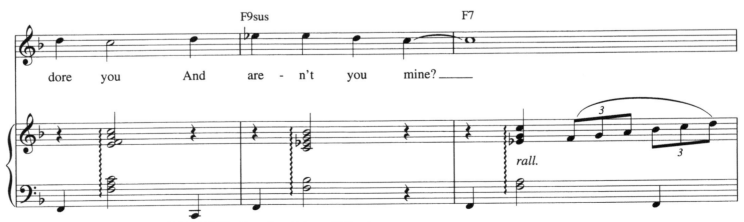

For the complete song see: HL00313101 *The Complete Cabaret Collection.*

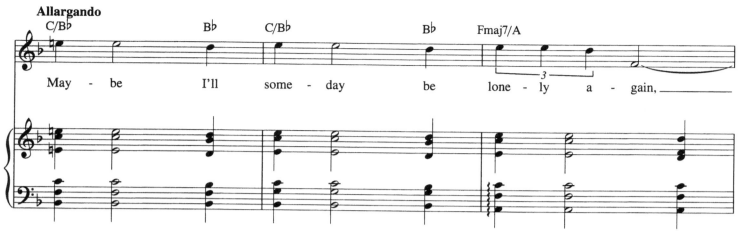

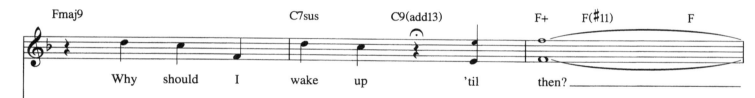

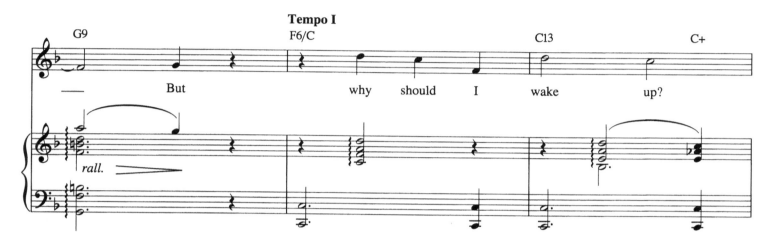

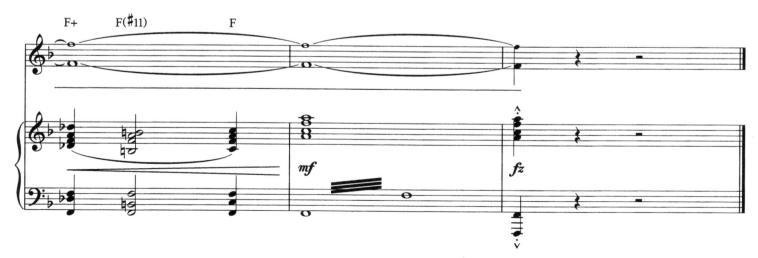

Excerpt

YESTERDAY

Words and Music by JOHN LENNON
and PAUL McCARTNEY

Moderately, with expression

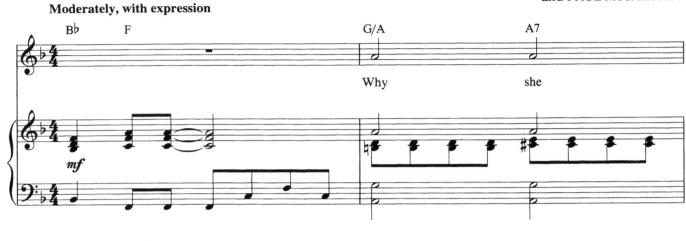

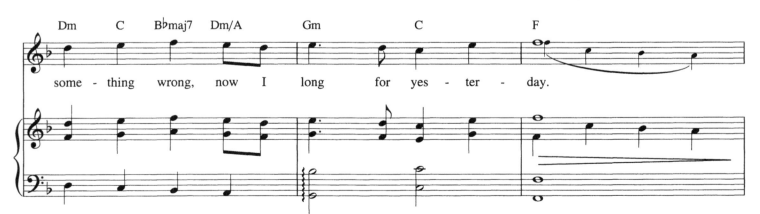

For the complete song see: HL00355735 *Yesterday* piano/vocal sheet music, and other sources.

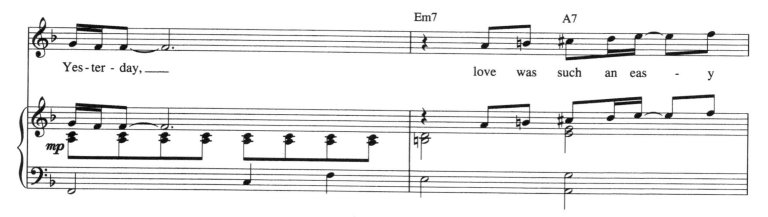

Yes-ter-day, ___ love was such an eas - y

game to play. ___ Now I need a place to

hide a - way, __ oh I be - lieve __ in yes - ter - day. __

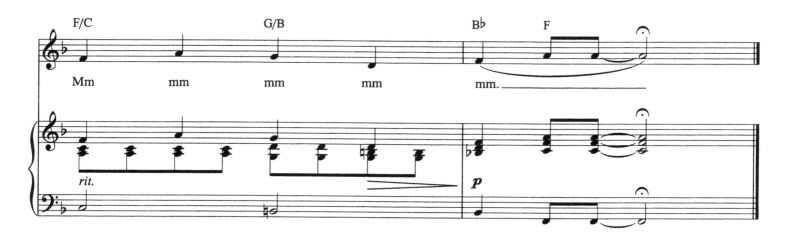

Mm mm mm mm mm. _____

YOU'RE NEVER FULL DRESSED WITHOUT A SMILE

from the Musical Production *Annie*

Lyric by MARTIN CHARNIN
Music by CHARLES STROUSE

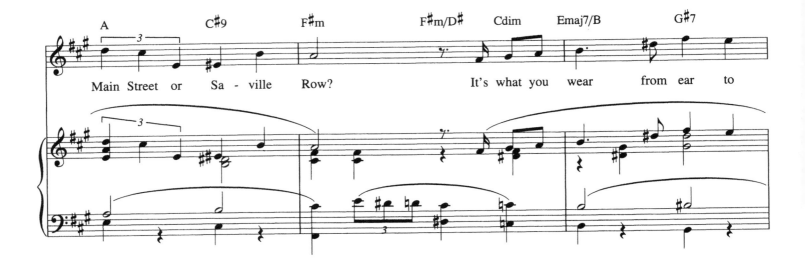

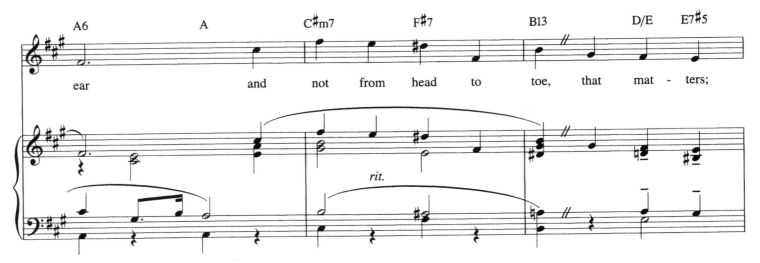

For the complete song see: HL00383056 *Annie* vocal selections, and other sources.

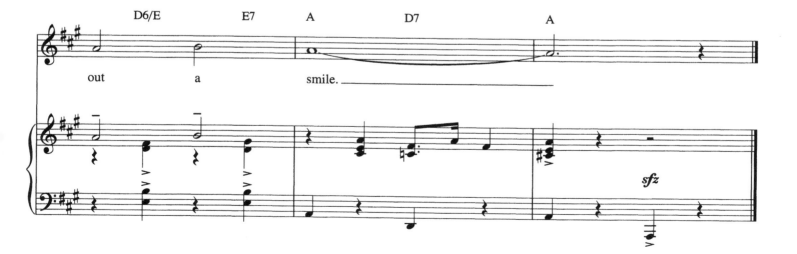

YOUNG AND FOOLISH
from *Plain and Fancy*

Words by ARNOLD B. HORWITT
Music by ALBERT HAGUE

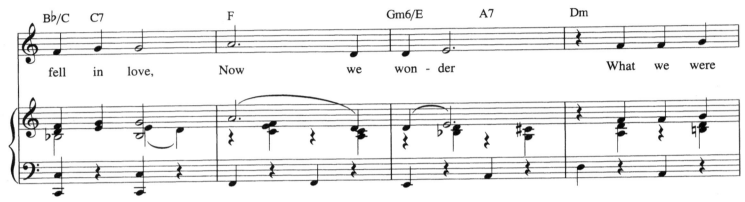

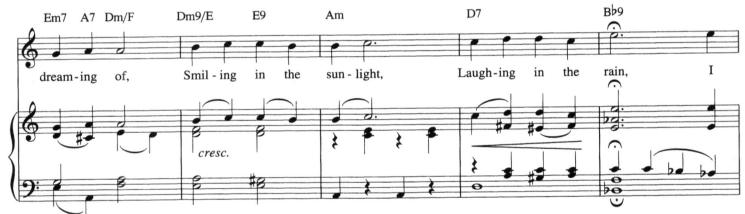

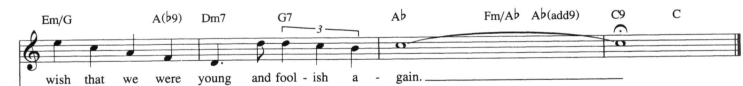

For the complete song see: HL00309245 *Broadway Deluxe,* and other sources.